GUITAR PRACTICE BY DESIGN

PRACTICE SECRETS OF THE PROS

TABLE OF CONTENTS

BEFORE YOU READ THIS BOOK...

PREFACE

How this book came to be.

My name is Coco Lee and Guitar Practice by Design: Practice Secrets of the Pros was born out of pure desperation. As you'll learn in this book, I was in a dark place in my life, and I felt like my purpose and destiny were slipping away.

Dreams of becoming a great guitarist and impacting the world with my music were fading into the distance. My dreams were on the brink of remaining my dreams. I was stuck. In debt. No money. No time. No progress. Then, I hit a breaking point.

It took me on an incredible journey of self-discovery and growth, which ultimately led me to uncover the secret frameworks that elite musicians and performers use to generate their success, among many other things.

The difference between you and the best musicians/performers in the world is simple: you're using different frameworks.

PRACTICE LIKE A BEGINNER. PLAY LIKE A BEGINNER.
PRACTICE LIKE A PRO. PLAY LIKE A PRO.

Change the framework - change the result.

The frameworks outlined in this book will help establish the pathway towards your dreams, but it's up to you to walk it.

This book is comprised of 4 smaller books which make up the complete series of Guitar Practice by Design: Practice Secrets of the Pros

- Decoded: Skill Building Secrets and Learning Hacks for Guitarists
- The Foolproof System for Easily Setting Goals and Gaining Achievement Momentum

- The Elite Framework for Practicing Like and Pro and Skyrocketing Progress
- The Guitarist's Guide to Total Practice Optimization: Biohacks and Blasting Through Plateaus

My goal is for this system to be the Foundation for your growth moving forward: unlocking your potential, becoming the guitarist you're destined to be, and changing the world with your music!

I decided to create this book because so many people struggle with making progress on guitar and often give up as a result. These lessons, and the information within, have helped me overcome every obstacle over my 20+ years of guitar experience, and I'm hoping that you can make this your Foundation to accomplish everything you've ever dreamed of on guitar.

I believe music is one of the most important things we have as a civilization. It allows us to connect unlike anything else. It's truly a universal language and has been a part of human culture since the dawn of time.

I don't want you to give up on guitar or music because you feel the road is too difficult or not worth it. I don't want you to give up on your dreams of being a musician, or potentially impacting the world with your music.

I don't want you to feel like you're not as 'talented' as other guitarists, or that they have something that you can't also have. I want you to understand that if someone else has accomplished something - you can as well. You just need the framework they operate from. That was my goal when writing this book; to put together the frameworks that the greatest musicians, guitarists, and performers use to create their exceptional results.

I want you to know that the road isn't difficult when you have a system; a blueprint. There are no shortcuts, but so much time is wasted being a guitarist that most people never reach their potential. Instead, we're hacking the process of practice and learning efficiently so that we can get the most out of the little time we do have. As a result, we're able to make more progress than we ever imagined possible.

I hope you enjoy this book and that it brings you clarity, excitement, and Motivation to conquer your goals. I genuinely believe in you, and I cannot wait to see what you're able to accomplish with this book.

By owning this book and utilizing its principles, you are now a **Practice Hacker**. Welcome to the elite group of musicians who are taking control of their musical destinies and creating extraordinary results without needing to practice all day long.

I would love to hear about your experiences with Guitar Practice by Design: Practice Secrets of the Pros.

Please email me with any stories, questions, concerns, or ideas at **info@ guitarpractice.design**

Your friend and fellow Practice Hacker,

    - COCO LEE

Introduction

I was born into a pretty musical family. My Mom and her Mother are singers and my Grandfather [on my Dad's side] was a country singer and guitarist. My Dad wasn't musically inclined, but he loved hard rock and metal bands from the 70s to 90s - so there was always music playing in the house. One band, in particular, was my Dad's favourite, which he played more than any other: KISS. Even as young as 2, I would be in front of the TV set, hopping around the living room, copying all of the moves.

But it wasn't until a particular moment that I truly knew I was meant to be a musician - specifically a guitarist, impacting the world in some way with my music.

His iconic look, the way he held the guitar and played - you would've thought this man was from outer space. Every note he played was telling an incredible story, the entire stadium was transported to his world. They were on a journey together. I was with them. Destination? Nobody knew. His guitar was pouring smoke and light, his soul was pouring out of every melody, every sci-fi sound effect. It was beyond remarkable, going on for what seemed like an eternity. Then it all came to a climax, and the song ended.

After coming back to earth, after the smoke settled, my mission became clear. Whatever I just witnessed, whatever that was - I needed to experience that. I needed to create something like that. I needed to impact people like that. I needed to become a guitarist. My destiny had revealed itself.

That performance was by Ace Frehley of KISS, the song was 'Shock Me'. It was a live taping from a performance in Houston in 1977. He had an extended guitar solo near the end of the song. To this very day, nothing I've heard comes CLOSE to the impact that had on me. I watched it over and over again. I'd copy every move - the way he'd play, the faces he made, pretending my guitar was smoking, even when he put down his guitar or blew it up and picked up another one. I knew every step. Every motion. I WAS Ace Frehley.

That memory stuck with me, even until now. It paved the Foundation for the path in life I wanted to walk. I knew I needed to create music like that - I needed to create an experience like that. The emotions I felt. The power. The transformation. I had to share that with others. I wanted to change the world. I wanted to help people with music. I wanted to inspire people. I needed this more than anything. I had to be on that stage.

I had no idea how I would get there, but I knew I had to do it.

I knew nothing else in life except that I wanted to be such a great guitarist that my music would have an impact on people like that.

As I got older [maybe 8 or 9], I got to pick up my first guitar thanks to a babysitter I had. She would always bring it over and even though it was never in tune and often missing strings, she knew I loved it. I would play all day and night when I could. I would stay up as late as possible writing songs complete with lyrics. I would pretend I was playing along to my favourite bands on MTV; Metallica, KISS, and even Limp Bizkit.

I was a guitarist. It was who I was. It's all I thought about. It's all I wanted to be.

I eventually got my own guitar, but without much direction or idea of where to go, I just kept playing and playing. Between the odd lessons, tab books, old 80s/90s rock guitar tapes [thanks Curt Mitchell], and eventually, YouTube when it came out, I was able to develop my skills to a pretty good level. This happens with most new hobbies. A lot of progress, quickly, even if the way you get there is ineffective. By the time I was around 13 or 14, I was able to play some riffs and songs by bands like Metallica, Ozzy Osbourne, Trivium, and Children of Bodom. I was also writing music of my own.

However, I hit a wall. I didn't know how to get past it. I don't know if it was ego, but I had this notion that as a guitarist, I had to figure everything out on my own. If I didn't get something right away, I would often give up or avoid it altogether. So I had no real way to 'improve' and my only practice strategy was to play for hours and hours on end.

I would just repeat the same riffs. I would never really push my comfort zone. I wasn't learning anything new. I was stuck. My body was getting used to the patterns, the speed, and the riffs. It had adapted, and I couldn't push it much further. I didn't know how to. I didn't even know where to look for answers. I just thought this was how it was. I just figured this was my 'skill level.'

I just needed more hours in the day… right?

Unfortunately, this issue continued for years after the fact. I never learned anything that pushed me. I never understood HOW to push myself and grow. Simply by playing for hours on end, I thought I was making progress. The problem is that I was starting to get older. As we all know, life begins to take on more responsibility and we lose more and more of that precious resource: time. But the real problem was that I was reactionary to my own life. I had dreams, sure, but I had no clear path towards them. Maybe you can relate.

Have you ever dreamed about something you wanted to accomplish, but it just stayed there, drifting in the clouds, no relevance to reality? Maybe that dream even began fading away - or left you completely?

I was stuck in dreamland, neglectful of other areas of my life, and as a result, everything spiralled out of control and hit rock bottom.

Here I was in my 20s, broke, in debt, living on my own, working full-time at a minimum wage job, and any 'free time' that I had wasn't going towards my craft. Yet, everyone around me was having success it seemed. I thought my time had passed. New guitarists were coming up that were changing the game. New music was coming out that was groundbreaking. I felt like I was meant to be a part of that, but I was stuck writing the same old songs, using the same old riffs and ideas, beating my head against a wall. How could all of these people be making progress and I'm not?

Are they just more talented than me?

Are they practicing more than me?

Was I starting to get too old?

I didn't get it.

I remember how I felt. I felt empty inside. Sad. Scared even. I felt like my soul was being sucked out of me. For the first time in my life, my purpose, my path, my reason for being was crumbling in front of me. Only a glimmer of light; of hope, was barely visible in what had now become a dark abyss. My dreams were slipping away. It was at this point that I knew I needed to change. Whatever I was doing wasn't working.

It was time for something new.

As they say in most recovery programs, the first step to recovery is awareness/acceptance of the problem. Well, I realized what the problem was. I knew why I wasn't making progress. It wasn't because others were more talented than me. It wasn't because I wasn't practicing enough. It wasn't because I was getting too old. It was simply ME.

My ignorance had been holding me back. It was my fault. My heart sank.

I wasn't actively engaging with my life. I wasn't even aware of how to. I was neglectful and my life suffered greatly because of it. I was repeating old behaviours and patterns and expecting new results. I was on a hamster wheel thinking I was in the race, how could I miss something so obvious? The truth really hurt.

The thing is, I always assumed I'd just make progress, but never thought about HOW I would make progress. That was the problem, and this happened in every area of my life: finances, relationships, education, health, music. I stopped making progress. I stopped engaging with my life. I became reactive, not proactive. I had no plan. I had no concrete goals. I wasn't Tracking anything. I wasn't in motion. I was hopelessly adrift in a vast sea of confusion and detachment, and I suffered because of it. I wish they taught you this stuff in school...

With this newly found awareness I knew that if I was the reason for my failure, I was going to be the reason for my success. I became aware of the problem, and now I had to fix it.

This revelation truly hit hard because of the pain it caused me for so long. All of those wasted years I would never get back. The potential success I could've had. Everything could've been different, but it wasn't. There I was, my purpose was fading away, and consequently, I was fading away. I had to do whatever it took to get myself out of suffering and back on my life purpose. I had no choice. I had to take control over my future or else I would live a life of regret, and it wouldn't just negatively affect *me*.

I genuinely believe that each individual has a unique hole to fill in this world that only THEY can fill. This is their purpose - no matter how big or small. I believe everyone has a unique calling in their life that can make the world a better place. But I also believe that if they don't fulfil it, it doesn't just become unrealized potential. It leaves a void in the world just as big as the unique hole they are meant to fill.

I knew that I was meant to do something with guitar and with music. I knew that if I didn't, I would suffer, and those I was meant to reach or impact in some way, big or small, would suffer as well. I feel this is true for every individual. So I had to do this for not only myself, but for those I was meant to potentially reach or impact in ways beyond my perception.

I couldn't accept the idea of my dreams remaining my dreams. Not trying, not progressing towards my goals was not an option. I want to get to the end of my life reflecting on everything that WAS - not what could've been. So from that moment forward, I knew that no matter what, I had to make this work. I didn't care what it took. I was going to make it happen.

The issue was, I didn't have more time to dedicate to guitar or any other area of my life, or at least, so I thought. So I had to figure out a way to get more out of the very little time I did have.

I didn't know what was possible. I didn't even really know where to look for answers. But whatever I was doing before wasn't working, so I was open to anything. I began searching for answers online and I eventually came across a certain YouTube channel that changed my life forever: Project Life Mastery.

That's when I was introduced to the world of personal development and self-improvement.

I would never be the same again.

It felt like I understood life for the first time. I don't know if you've had an experience like that before, but it was like being unplugged from the Matrix. I saw everything differently. I saw how it all connected in ways I was blind to before. I saw the underlying nature of life. I saw how all of my previous mistakes could've been avoided, and I saw how my future could be created. I felt like I had accessed sacred information that was taboo, illegal, or forbidden. It truly felt that surreal and powerful. Yet it was all so obvious and simple.

I consumed all of the content I could. I immersed myself in all of the videos on his channel and others that I could find. It was like every false belief I had was being broken. I felt renewed. Anything was possible. I remember going to work with a binder and writing notes extensively on my lunch-breaks. I would wake up every morning at 4:00/4:30am. I would try to fit in a morning routine and study before I went to work, and the second I got home, I would study until I went to bed. I dedicated every waking moment I had to self-improvement. As a result, my life and potential began to unfold in ways that I never would have imagined.

I was so excited - it truly felt like a second chance. I could create the life I always dreamed of. I was no longer ignorant. I could now take control of my destiny. But it required something I hadn't considered before...

What do successful people have that the average person doesn't?

- More Talent?
- More Luck?
- Better Genes?
- More Intelligence?
- More Money?
- More Status?

While some of these might appear to be true or important, they aren't key factors.

Consider this:

- Chefs can spend their entire lives studying and improving the art of cooking. Through trial and error, they develop recipes, techniques, and systems that create their current results.
- You would think that simply having more time in the kitchen would produce world-class results, right? Wrong.
- If one of the world's top chefs were to teach a brand new chef everything they knew, the Foundation of the new chef would start from the Pinnacle of all of the wisdom and experience of that top chef.
- Consequently, within a very short time, they would be able to out-do most other chefs and be able to compete with their mentor, the top chef.
- Did they need an entire lifetime to gain that experience? No. They made the Pinnacle of the top chef their Foundation.
- Compare that to a chef who tried learning everything on their own, or got caught in bad habits. There would be little to no progress, even with MANY more years involved.

What's the key difference here? Simply put, the frameworks they follow determine the results they get.

To create success, you must emulate successful frameworks. If you don't have success now - it's because you're following a framework that doesn't produce success. It's like having a map. You might eventually figure out what roads to take by going along them, making the wrong turns, running out of gas, backtracking, and then EVENTUALLY getting there. Or, you can follow a clear map from someone who has travelled the path, to get from A to B with ease, and then explore further beyond that.

It's really that simple.

One of the quickest ways to emulate success is by Making the Pinnacle of Others Your Foundation [which is described in-depth in **Secret 2**]. How are they thinking differently? What Beliefs do they have that support their success? How do they view life? What techniques, knowledge, procedures, etc., have they developed and now use to produce successful results? What are their frameworks? What have they learned? Instead of trying to reinvent the wheel, integrate the success of others into your Foundation and build towards greater potential.

This realization was a game changer for me and it led me to think about how this applied to guitar. For so long, I was following the Old Framework:

- To be great, you need to put in more time, you need to practice more [while the rest of your life suffers as a result].

- Focuses on the 'what' of learning, not the 'how' [gives the illusion of progress while actually holding you back].

- Progress happens slowly, even with lessons [wasting thousands of dollars, and hundreds of hours a year ineffectively practicing].

- Doesn't address the root cause of your limitations [wasting your time, building destructive habits, and creating vast imbalances in your playing].

- Only engages the Skill Development Zone, which is solely responsible for progress, for 3-6 minutes per 60-minute practice session on average [the rest is wasted time, energy, and money].

- Holds you back from your potential [making it impossible to become the guitarist you've always dreamed of being and impacting the world with your music].

If this framework worked, wouldn't everyone be an elite guitarist?

No wonder I was stuck...

Practice like a Beginner, Play like a Beginner

I knew that the key to success was to emulate what produced success. But there was already a LOT of information out there on *what* to practice on guitar. Scales, modes, licks, riffs, different types of picking, songs, etc. Millions of teachers and resources all showing some cool trick or fun pattern.

Then it hit me. And hard.

There is a copious amount of information on WHAT to practice, but basically nothing on HOW to practice.

If I wanted to Play like a Pro, I needed to Practice like a Pro

Which led me to ask myself: how were the best guitarists and musicians practicing to get their results?

What were they doing that I wasn't?

I knew it wasn't just talent or luck or any of those previous false beliefs I had. Clearly, they were following a system; a framework that produced those results. Something they likely developed over time and maybe they weren't even fully aware of it. But it was a refined framework that produced elite-level results. I realized that to truly make progress and become the guitarist I dreamed of being, I needed to discover these frameworks and begin using them as my Foundation NOW. I had a lot of time to make up for...

I want to provide you with an analogy as to why this is such a critical concept.

Elite athletes don't work out for 10 hours a day. Many of them only work out for 1-2 hours max, though there are always exceptions. They don't just show up and do random exercises hoping to grow. They follow very specific training plans, optimizing every movement, every rep, every set, and every rest period. They even optimize their diet and sleep. They have a clear Vision of what they want. They set Goals, and they stay on track towards accomplishing them. They understand the mechanics behind creating growth, and focus only around those - wasting as little time and energy as possible. Then, they adjust when they hit plateaus to continue progressing.

Compare that to the average gym-goer.

They have no plan. They do a few exercises. They show up on random days, for varying periods. There's no real purpose. Sure they want to lose weight or gain muscle but lack understanding of how to make it happen.

The difference between the two? You can say genetics, you can say talent, but the REAL difference? The framework. Their frameworks are producing their results. So how can the average gym-goer get elite results? Start using an elite framework - the plans, the movements, the optimization, the mindset, the Beliefs, the Vision, the education, the understanding, the diet, the nutrition, etc.

Seems pretty obvious right? Well, how is it that music is approached in the opposite way?

We just assume that to make progress we must play and practice more and we'll eventually get there. That's just simply not true, and in my opinion, it's a dangerous and haphazard approach. That process, over time [if we're lucky], helps us refine and create a better framework, sure.

But if we continue with ineffective methods, we'll get the same results over and over again, never improving. Worse, we'll often develop really bad habits because of this approach, which makes progress that much harder to attain.

What if you had the frameworks that are responsible for the success of the greatest guitarists, musicians, and performers in the world? What if you had the frameworks that were responsible for elite-level results? The Mindset, the Beliefs, the Vision, the strategies, and the ways to properly push and stimulate the mind and body to achieve maximum results in minimal time? What if you had the best ways to track, optimize, and blast through plateaus?

My biggest worry is that most musicians don't figure these frameworks out in time, if at all. Because of their struggle to make progress, they don't reach their potential. Even worse, they don't fulfil their unique purpose in the world - even giving up guitar or music entirely.

How many guitarists or musicians do you know that have given up or quit because it's 'too difficult?' Or that they've been playing so long, but haven't improved - so it's just not worth the time, effort, and money anymore? Maybe you're even one of those guitarists.

That kills me. Honestly, it does, because I've been there. I almost gave up as well.

But there's another way.

I knew I had to find a solution to this problem. There had to be a core framework that these elite guitarists and performers were using to create their results. Even if they were unaware of it and developed it more or less intuitively, they were following a system. It wasn't just random. It wasn't just chance. That system is the difference between them, and us.

The problem is that as musicians, we're very creative but often not very logical or analytical. We might learn strategies from teachers, or develop ideas over time, but mostly, these systems become internalized and we're not always aware of what makes them work.

So I knew that to discover the core framework responsible for creating elite-level results as a musician, I had to go deeper.

- I researched the frameworks and practice routines of my favourite guitarists as well as high-performing artists, musicians, and performers.
- I read the best books I could find on the science of learning and practice. Books on developing, and mastering new skills. On self-improvement. On success habits. On psychology. Whatever I could find related to the subject of self-mastery.
- I studied the best scientific research I could find on music practice, strategies, and self-regulation.
- I read countless articles, listened to numerous podcasts and interviews, watched hundreds of videos and much more.

Through all of this research and testing, I found it. I discovered the unified framework that produced elite results. I understood what set these individuals apart from the average person. I discovered **The Practice Secrets of the Pros.** Throughout the rest of this book, I'll be teaching you this framework; this system.

It will go through:

- Fundamentals of Skill Building
- 3 Fundamental Aspects of Guitar
- The Science of Learning
- Practice Strategies including the 4 Pillars of Practicology
- Mindset and Beliefs
- Developing your Vision [Macro and Micro]
- Effective Goal-Setting
- Daily Routine and Weekly Sequencing
- Preparing for Practice
- The Elite Framework

- Tracking and Analysis
- Breaking Through to the Next Level

My path is still constantly evolving. I'm not perfect. I'm still growing and learning. We all are. And even in mastery, there is always more to learn. We can always become more - this is an amazing part of life.

But I now have the framework that produces elite-level results. It has allowed me to become the guitarist I've always dreamed of being, without needing to practice all day long. It's a system that maximizes output and minimizes input. That optimizes each session around creating growth and progress. I don't have to guess anymore. I don't need to worry if what I'm doing is working. I know that I'm growing. And every part of my life has improved as a result.

The freedom, the joy, and the happiness that I feel after all of these years is immeasurable.

I was stuck, I felt like I couldn't move forward with my music goals, I couldn't improve with guitar but now, I feel like I truly have unlimited potential. I can focus on my path with music and in life knowing I'm no longer held back by my ignorance and inability to make progress on guitar.

I've been able to improve every element of my playing substantially. Whether it's speed, mastering a certain Technique, increasing the efficiency and fluidity of my playing, improving my timing, being able to express each note and phrase more accurately, or anything else you can imagine. I've been able to easily and quickly fix all of my problems, becoming the guitarist I've always dreamed of being.

My songwriting and Creativity has improved dramatically, being able to learn and implement new Theory and new Techniques with ease. I'm also able to write faster and improvise better, easily integrating new ideas as they happen through the processes you'll learn in this book.

Introduction

My lead playing has improved exponentially - the overall quality of my solos, the melodies, the Techniques, and the emotion are at an all-time high for me. I'm also the tightest rhythm player I've ever been. I feel like I have complete control over every single note, every accent, and every bit of nuance to my playing.

One of the coolest benefits of all of this growth is that I'm now able to learn new songs very quickly, which was something I always struggled with. It's why I never really bothered to learn new music before - my ego wouldn't have it. I couldn't do it as well as other things, so I never really tried. And now it's easy for me.

The list goes on. I'm not trying to make this all about myself, but I really want to drive the point home. I want you to know that these frameworks really work and they have impacted me in ways I can't fully express, and I feel like I can accomplish anything musically now. This process has helped me become a better musician, and a better person.

I went from struggling for so long on guitar [and in life] and doing the same things over and over again [using the Old Framework], to taking control of my musical destiny. I'm able to play or learn anything I desire. I'm able to create the music I've always wanted to create. I don't need to spend every hour of the day practicing. I know HOW to practice and what to practice to get the results I desire. I have the Practice Secrets of the Pros. And it has changed my life.

The incredible thing is that the principles in this book go beyond just guitar - they apply to life. In fact, the most successful people [regardless of profession] all have a similar approach to life - they operate from a similar framework. As I was searching for answers to my guitar practice problems, I uncovered so much information that was almost more important than the practice itself and I knew I had to include it in this book. It was critical.

In a sense, this is a sort of like a self-development guide for guitarists - helping cultivate the person you're destined to be; the guitarist of your dreams. It prepares you to most effectively use The Elite Framework which is the primary system that creates progress on guitar. It's truly the secret sauce.

With the Practice Secrets of the Pros now I can focus on creating and performing music without the limitations I once had. I feel my entire future has opened up and I can truly begin to walk the path. Most importantly, I get to share everything I have learned and discovered with you. That's what I'm most excited about.

I created this book for you.

I hope that you don't have to suffer any longer and that you don't have to give up or struggle with progress from now on. I truly hope that you can become the guitarist you've always dreamed of being - whatever that is to you, without limitation. And, hopefully in that process, you're able to become a greater participant in your own life, allowing more doors and opportunities to open up for you.

You've been following the Old Framework that no longer serves you.

Now, you have the New Framework. You have The Elite Framework. You have the Practice Secrets of the Pros. Make this your Foundation.

Become your potential. Become more.

The future is yours, **Practice Hacker**, and I can't wait to see what you do with it.

PRACTICE HACKER MANIFESTO

A Practice Hacker is someone who desires to become the guitarist of their dreams without needing to practice all day long.

Who doesn't use excuses, they use what they have.

Who desires to fulfill their unique purpose in the world, impacting others with their music.

Who Makes the Pinnacle of Other Their Foundation.

A Practice Hacker accelerates their pathway to mastery by creating with what they are learning.

Who uses The Elite Framework to engage the Skill Development Zone for their entire practice session - getting 10-20x the results.

Who minimizes input while maximizing output.

Who is obsessed with growth and learning, and does whatever it takes to make their dreams a reality.

A Practice Hacker is a master of self-regulation; focusing on what produces results while quickly addressing and fixing what doesn't.

And they love to share their knowledge and wisdom with others.

———

Become your potential. Become more.

You're Only One Practice Away...

BOOK I

DECODED: SKILL BUILDING SECRETS AND LEARNING HACKS FOR GUITARISTS

FUNDAMENTALS OF SKILL BUILDING

Secret 1

Pinnacle/Foundation Theory

Hour after hour, day after day I practiced. I was putting so much time in, so why wasn't I making progress? What was I doing wrong? I thought I was learning all of the right things: scales, modes, chords, techniques. I was trying to figure out how to practice more effectively, yet nothing was really changing. Whatever I was doing wasn't working anymore. I knew I had to go back to the beginning - even beyond just the basics of Technique or Theory. I needed to understand how to learn.

In my search to understand how to learn, I began consuming a lot of different content: YouTube videos, podcasts, articles, and books. One day, I was listening to a Tim Ferriss podcast and he was interviewing a man named Josh Waitzkin. They were discussing his book 'The Art of Learning' and I remember I was completely blown away by the concepts he spoke of and his story. I had to listen to the podcast multiple times, and took a lot of notes. I knew I had to get his book.

It went over concepts I had been coming to understand and was developing somewhat intuitively. I had begun to see things in a certain way in my head, but I thought that was just how I understood them. However, the way he was explaining them was like he was seeing them in a similar way. He was speaking my language. And upon diving in deeper, it addressed a major issue I had.

My entire previous understanding and approach were wrong: I was trying to learn all of these disconnected ideas without first developing a Foundation. I needed a structured way to build skills and develop them. Through my experiences, research, and many of the concepts in his book, I synthesized an idea I call **Pinnacle/Foundation Theory**.

The concept is simple: with any form of skill development, you must start by establishing the Foundation. You then want to internalize the Foundation so it becomes automatic and you want to continue building until you reach a Pinnacle. The Pinnacle holds all of the information that has built up to it, yet you only need to engage with the Pinnacle to use all of it. The amazing thing is that once this Pinnacle is developed, it becomes a part of the Foundation for the next level. Pinnacles become new Foundations.

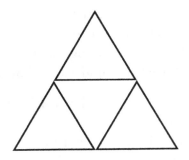

This not only opened me up to a better understanding of how I should be building skills, but also helped me better understand how to develop a pathway for myself - in what order or sequence I should learn. You don't know what you don't know. But if you begin with the basics [Foundation], you increase your knowledge and your ability.

By integrating and automating the Foundation, you'll begin to build towards a Pinnacle. Inevitably, you'll come to understand your limits, and you'll have better questions to ask yourself in order to find the answers.

This is why awareness of the process is key. Each level you improve and build upon, you'll gain more clarity and you'll be able to see a bit further along your path.

A good example is being at the base of a mountain. You might see the Pinnacle from the base, but your vision is very limited. You won't truly understand how high up it is, what types of obstacles will be in your way, or what's beyond it until you move further up the mountain. When you're at the halfway point, your perspective is suddenly much clearer. You have the wisdom of the travel that brought you up there, which is real concrete understanding gained through knowledge and experience. Additionally, you have a greater depth of vision for the rest of the ascent - and even what potentially lies beyond. This will only improve as you move further up the mountain.

Then once you reach the top of the mountain, all of the wisdom [knowledge + experience] that brought you up there now exists at the Pinnacle. This then becomes your new Foundation, allowing for greater frontiers to be explored. The wisdom of what came before integrated and automated. It's now a part of you.

Compare that to trying to assume what's at the top from the base of the mountain. You won't be able to. You can take the wisdom of others and use that as your Foundation [which we will explain in the next chapter] but if you do this on your own you'll likely struggle. This is because you lack the knowledge to get you to where you need to go.

When starting at a high-level concept, it's very difficult to even know where to begin. Start at the most basic Foundation you need, and build it up correctly. The better you do this, the better you'll be able to self-regulate your journey [which is a critical part of this book]. You'll have better questions to ask, and you'll have a better understanding of where to find information [or even what to look for].

Here's an example as it relates to guitar:

- Imagine you're a brand new guitarist - you have no idea where to begin. Imagine if you tried learning a technically demanding song by Jason Richardson. You would struggle. You wouldn't really know how to hold the pick, how to hold the guitar, the correct pick movements, the ideal picking angle, note quality, accuracy, timing, etc. It's starting at a pretty high-level concept if you're brand new. Maybe after a long time you could figure it out, bit-by-bit. Maybe you could slowly build up to it. But how effective do you think this process is? How much wasted time would there be?

- Alternatively, what if you started by working on those fundamental skills [even using that song as a reference], building your Foundations first? Learning how to pick, learning how to fret, working on the basics of timing and note quality? Then once those basics [Foundations] are better internalized, you build them [creating Pinnacles] and combine them with other skills [creating new Foundations] to build to the level needed to learn the song. These skills would be developed faster, and would have more applications. Plus, you wouldn't get so discouraged early on. A much better approach!

To become a master, you must develop the fundamentals, integrate them, expand outwards, and repeat. Each level of progress must become internalized - it must become automatic. The Foundation must build into a Pinnacle, and that Pinnacle must become the Foundation for the next level, further internalized - ever expanding.

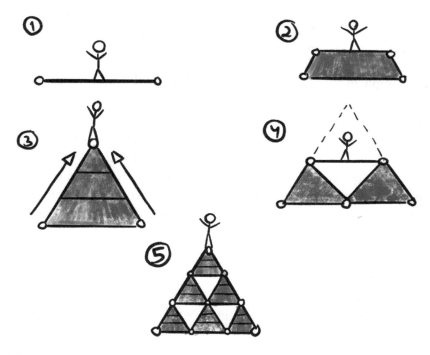

[1] First, you start with the Foundation. [2] By Encoding, you build an integrated base, which heightens the Foundation. [3] Repeat this until you build a Pinnacle which holds all information within. [4] The Pinnacle then becomes the Foundation for the next level and so the cycle repeats until you've [5] built up highly complex and perfected skills from rudimentary and basic Foundations.

STEP #1: FOUNDATION

To build the Foundation, you need to understand what the fundamentals are - the basics. Work on them individually, or as needed. Here, experience is gained through applied knowledge which creates understanding [wisdom].

You need to ensure the Foundation is strong and well integrated. It makes the rest of the process a lot easier and you don't have to come back to fix mistakes. Even if you're a more experienced guitarist, I highly recommend going back to the basics you've missed if you really want to master your craft. You'll know if certain things are holding you back. Humble yourself. We all have more to learn.

An example of this would be in terms of Theory. If you have no idea what the modes are, but you know one scale in and out, your playing will be limited to that scale. Sure, you might know that one scale very well, and be able to explore other sounds or ideas around it, but you're limited in your ability to write, to solo, to improvise, and ultimately - to create. However, you don't need to master everything. You want to focus on your strengths, and bring up your Foundation to support them. A weak Foundation will only become more unstable, eventually collapsing the higher you build.

STEP #2: ENCODING

The process of Encoding is the process where understanding becomes automated and integrated through perfected repetition.

Think of any new skill you've learned before - even walking as a small child. First, you start with the basic motions or ideas of it. Once you establish them through perfected repetition, they become internalized, and you're able to go a bit further with their applications. The quicker you can perfect the repetition, the quicker you can Encode it, and therefore the quicker you can build off of it.

This is why it's beneficial early on to have a mentor or teacher who understands what the Foundations are and what perfected repetition looks like. But practice is a form of self-regulated learning - so a teacher can only go so far. You need to improve your self-regulation abilities. The better they are, the better you can address issues, fix them, Encode them, and build towards perfection.

The issue is that in most cases we aren't really aware of this process. On guitar, there's a specific approach to building skills that we'll go over in The Elite Framework. However, the idea is simple: we want to build our skills and abilities by integrating each step to get there. If we max out at playing at 100bpm, we want to properly Encode the movements at 100bpm so they become internalized and they become our new Foundation. Then we can focus on 110bpm, 130bpm, and more.

Most guitar practice sessions rarely Encode properly, and certainly not in a way that pushes what I call the Skill Development Zone which we will discuss later. However, The Elite Framework is solely built around both. But, for now just realize that building Foundations into Pinnacles is through the process of Encoding - perfected repetition.

STEP #3: PINNACLE

Through layers of Encoding, understanding builds into a Pinnacle which is the final Encoding for that level or application of the skill. Within it lies all of the previous levels you've Encoded. They are all internalized. They are automatic.

Think of the power that an elite boxer or MMA fighter has in a single punch. Why is that? They have practiced their strikes so much, to such a perfected degree, that they are able to maximize their output of the punch while minimizing the movement [and wasted energy]. All of their previous experience and application has hyper-developed that particular movement. One motion holds hundreds if not thousands of perfected repetitions.

> "I fear not the man who has practiced 10,000 kicks once, but I fear the man who has practiced one kick 10,000 times."
>
> - BRUCE LEE

STEP #4: CREATE NEW FOUNDATIONS

Now, with the newly formed Pinnacle, it can become the Foundation for the next level. The entire previous body of knowledge [now wisdom] is held within that single point, thus allowing for greater levels and greater applications of the skill.

Consider if you're learning basic skills. First, you learn how to pick properly. Then you might learn how to alternate pick. Then you might build up speed and clarity, as well as efficiency and fluidity. Then you might work on different scales, patterns, and movements - applying that skill. After all that, you might infuse other Techniques and applications. These all build off of each other and require strong Foundations, which become Pinnacles, which in turn become new Foundations.

STEP #5: EXPAND

Repeat the previous steps as needed to develop the desired skill and its applications - further integrating and automating each level as you need. This sequence of learning often opens up understanding and insight into what the next level of your path might hold. This is applicable to many aspects of life.

This is an example of how each Pinnacle/Foundation branches out, forming new structures, and creating new pathways. It's meant to give you an idea of how simplicity can expand into complexity - its core being a strong, developed Foundation.

HOW TO APPLY THIS

The process of skill development happens automatically for most people, usually as a form of reaction to external stimulus. The problem is that most education and skill development stops or greatly decreases when people leave school or a place where this stimulation happens. They are usually reactionary.

To truly gain mastery you must become proactive with your own path, and therefore with how you learn. You need to become aware of the nature of skill development. Whenever you approach any new skill, in guitar or not, the process isn't complex. Many people give up because it's 'too hard.' The reason it's too hard is that they are starting at too high of a Pinnacle, with their Foundation still many levels below. Starting at the correct Foundation, and building up through proper Encoding will allow much greater ease in accomplishing what previously seemed impossible. It's about incremental steps that build off each other. These steps will eventually compound over time and allow for exponential growth across multiple areas.

So, if you struggle with something new, don't get discouraged. You're simply approaching something you haven't quite developed up to yet. If you're able to identify your Foundation and where you want to go [start as basic as you need to], you can take the necessary steps to get there with far greater ease and confidence. Each step you take, you'll see a bit further beyond, and you'll be all the more wise.

> **Practice Hacker Tip:** Understand and actively engage with the nature of skill development. It simplifies and focuses your efforts in building towards greater perfection without wondering if what you're doing is working.

Secret 2

Make the Pinnacle of Others Your Foundation

[1] First you start with the Foundation. [2] By Making the Pinnacle of Others Your Foundation, you take the expert's entire lifetime of experience; of trial and error, and you pick up from where they left off. [3] This becomes your new Foundation and allows quicker progression of your path.

Years ago, during the time when I hit rock bottom, one of the key realizations I gained was that my results were because of my framework. This was made even clearer by the book Unlimited Power from Tony Robbins. For so long, I thought I could do everything myself. In fact,

I took pride in that. I truly believed I was supposed to do it that way. I was proud that I was self-taught. I was proud that I only played my own songs and I didn't learn other people's songs. I had all these notions of what it meant to be a great guitarist when in reality, they held me back from being one.

So when this realization hit me, I knew I needed a New Framework. I needed a new way to approach guitar. I needed a new way to approach life.

I had to figure out what the top musicians, guitarists, and performers were doing to create their exceptional results. I needed to understand their frameworks. Some people dedicate their entire lives to mastery in a given subject. They took what came before them, made it their Foundation, and then pushed the boundaries forward.

Yet I was doing the opposite...

I wasn't using what came before me as my Foundation. I wasn't pushing anything forward. I was too busy trying to start from ground zero, reinventing the wheel. I was struggling, on my own, somehow thinking that was the right way. It's no surprise I wasn't making progress.

This was a massive shift that needed to happen in me, but I was desperate for answers to my problems. Once I fixed this, it opened up my entire guitar journey to me. Actually, it opened up my entire life. It was a new beginning and one that was able to actually push me forward. To really make progress, you need to learn and integrate the wisdom of those before you; Making the Pinnacle of Others Your Foundation.

FOUNDATION

When learning a new skill, it's incredibly helpful to start with expert knowledge. However, in some cases, just learning something academically without understanding and experiencing its applications can limit your learning.

This is why you should first test your abilities and knowledge by approaching the new Foundation and seeing what you're capable of with what you currently know. This can help establish a connection between what you know and don't know and will allow for Expert Modelling to fill in the blanks. Approach something new and see how far you can get.

Doing it this way is like leaving an open-ended question for your mind to answer. Or it's like reading the questions for a test before studying for it; it will prepare your mind to fill in what's missing, helping you find the answers, or even help you ask better questions in your search for answers.

EXPERT MODELLING

Depending on what your Foundation is, there are different experts on the topic. Do some basic research to find them - ideally people in your preferred genre or niche of music. You likely already know them. They are probably your favourite guitarists or guitarists you know of that are exceptional at what they do.

They can become the masters you wish to emulate. Their frameworks will usually exist in video or book form, perhaps even an article or podcast. Books, videos, and even podcasts are preferable as more information can be conveyed. One thing to keep in mind though is that musicians are creative, intuitive, and often not very rational or logical. So they might tell you to practice for 10 hours a day or to just 'play' and you'll eventually get it. However, there are real mechanisms at play that are creating growth, even if they aren't articulating them. Try to find those. If they are using blanket statements like 'play more,' take it with a grain of salt and look deeper.

Successful habits produce successful results, so observe these across every dimension you can. Every bit will help you.

The Pinnacle of others will open up your basic level of understanding and allow you to ask yourself better questions. Integrate these ideas as your new Foundation.

MASTERY AND WHAT COMES NEXT

True mastery comes from integrating the wisdom that has come before, making it your Foundation, and pushing into brand new territories. This is where innovation, progress, and evolution takes place. With these new internalized ideas, you'll have a better understanding of what should come next in your journey. You'll have better questions to ask yourself, and you'll know what's missing or at least where to look.

As stated earlier, don't seek to master everything, but also don't hyper-focus on just mastering one thing.

PILLAR OF SPECIALIZATION

You should have a unique approach or focus that sets you apart and becomes your specialty. This can be a certain approach to writing, melodic or harmonic composition, a signature lead style, a certain Technique, a certain genre, etc.

As you pursue Specialization, you'll need to establish higher Foundations to support growth and exploration. To build the Pillars, you must have a strong Foundation, and the Pillars can only go as high as the Foundation allows. Learn what's necessary for you - go as deep as you want in a given area based on your desired outcome. Make the Pinnacle of Others Your Foundation, and focus on your unique approach or contribution to music and guitar [Pillar of Specialization]. Find what excites you, and use that as your guide.

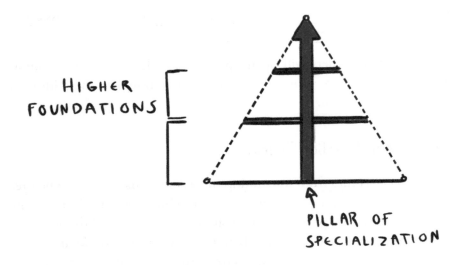

The Pillar of Specialization guides your journey and your Foundation supports it. As you raise your Foundation, your Pillar can go further. They rely on each other. They cannot truly excel or progress without each other. Neglect one and the other will fall.

Not every Pinnacle will form a new Foundation you can easily recognize, and you might not always understand where to go next based on your Goals. To make this process a bit easier, I designed a chart called **Pathway by Design**. It is a map that covers the 3 Fundamental Aspects of Guitar [that we will be going over in the next chapter] and shows you potential pathways, sequences, and connections of skills.

The point isn't to learn and master EVERY single aspect of guitar, but you want to develop a strong enough Foundation to support your Pillar of Specialization. You don't want to waste time and energy in areas that don't serve you, but you also don't want to waste time hyper-focusing on one area, neglecting things that are necessary to support its growth.

HOW TO APPLY THIS

Being able to effectively build your Foundation is key. You want to build your Pillar of Specialization to master a given area, but you also need to develop higher Foundations to support it. Don't try to reinvent the wheel or do everything yourself. Make the Pinnacle of Others Your Foundation.

To simplify this process:

- Establish where your Foundation is - see what you're capable of when learning something. See where your weak points are. Get familiar with the basics.

- Find experts who have mastered these Foundations to accelerate your progress. Make their Pinnacle your Foundation; integrate their knowledge and push it forward into new territory.

- Learn to ask better questions, and you'll discover better answers. More specific questions provoke more specific answers.

- Consider picking up **Pathway by Design**, if you haven't already, for a higher-level overview of potential pathways you can take along your journey. This will only make the process clearer, easier, and quicker.

Practice Hacker Tip: Focus on your Pillar of Specialization and continue to raise your Foundation by Making The Pinnacle of Others Your Foundation.

Secret 3

The 3 Fundamental Aspects of Guitar

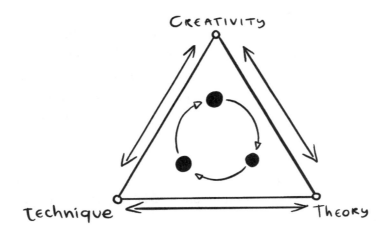

The 3 Fundamental Aspects of Guitar guide, inform, and influence each other. They must operate in Synergy for you to truly benefit and grow. The sum is greater than its parts.

So now I knew to truly make progress, I needed to Make the Pinnacle of Others my Foundation. But I also knew that if I started from too high of a Pinnacle, everything would collapse. So I had to discover what the absolute Foundations were for guitar. What main areas did all skills and pathways stem from? I concluded that the 3 Fundamental Aspects of Guitar are Technique, Theory, and Creativity.

Some might argue that you can divide this differently, including or prioritizing skills like ear-training, improvisation, or sight-reading. But basically any skill can fit into 1 or more of these 3 categories. However, the 3 I listed have quite different approaches and are critical to develop if you truly seek mastery. With this framework, my goal is to provide a basic system of how such learning works. Each approach and application will be a bit different depending on the person and their unique path. Consider this teaching you how to fish, instead of simply giving you a fish.

TECHNIQUE

With Technique, you want to first identify the physical requirements of the skill you're approaching, and you need to identify the proper Performance Measurements needed to play it perfectly [more on this in **Secret 7**]. If you don't do this, you can't build Technique and you'll quickly reach limits.

To build the Foundation, it depends on where you are starting, but understanding how the different Techniques connect can truly help. This is where **Pathway by Design** comes into play. Regardless, even if you're new to a concept like alternate picking, you wouldn't start with all of its high-level applications or modified Techniques [economy picking, hybrid picking, etc.].

You would start with the basics of alternate picking as the Foundation first - learning and perfecting the physical requirements before moving on to greater applications.

Wherever your starting point, you just need to Encode through perfected repetition, ensuring that you're integrating and automating each level with as much efficiency as possible so you can easily build up speed and further applications.

THEORY

Theory is very similar to Technique in how you approach learning it, but the actual learning process is more about coming to understand and applying the Theory. As you apply Theory, you'll be using Technique so it will still go through the same sequence for building Foundations into Pinnacles.

We're not approaching Theory from a purely academic sense - though if that's what you want to do, that's fine. But for me, it's about the application and real use. I see Theory as the language of music. It's a way for us to communicate, organize, and further explore musical landscapes and ideas.

With that being said, you still want to start with the basics - establish a strong Foundation. Even if you know bits and pieces now, it will hold you back if your Foundation is weak. You don't have to master every bit of Theory. You don't need to learn how to play perfectly in every single key or know every single mode or scale ever. But if you want to learn and use Theory, you should begin with the basics so you have a solid Foundation.

CREATIVITY

We will be discussing Creativity quite a bit throughout this book. It's quite an interesting concept.

Your level of Technique and Theory will open up greater potential for creative ideas. However, Creativity is also a state which is influenced by different factors: Inspiration, Motivation, environment, Beliefs, Mindset, health, etc. Your Foundation will determine how well you're able to express and articulate creative ideas - as well as the level and quality of them.

Have you ever composed or heard an amazing song in your head that's unlike anything you've heard before? But when you tried to play it and figure it out, you couldn't? Or maybe you were really advanced in a certain Technique or aspects of Theory but you couldn't express much Creativity with it?

This is an example of this discrepancy. Both sides of Creativity need to work together. Technique and Theory will develop Creativity, and your development of Creativity will further develop Technique and Theory.

The more you push one, the more you'll need to push the other. Thus is the dance of progress.

SYNERGY

Like a painter, true mastery doesn't lie within specific Techniques or Theory, it's through the vision you are expressing. It's the ability to most accurately explore and depict your creative vision without limitation. True mastery is using what's needed, not what's fancy or impressive to others.

> We want to **become the painting** - not the painter
> We want to **serve the creative vision** - not the ego

This is the ultimate goal, in my opinion. Technique and Theory are tools that will help you access, explore, and materialize Creativity in a way that can fully express the way you experience it. Like being able to explore a new world or a new universe and being able to invite other people into it.

This is one of the most amazing parts of being an artist or musician. You move into the unknown, into the transcendent, into the abstract, and you explore its depths. You learn, you grow, and you experience transformation - coming back a little bit different than you were before, with something new to offer the world. You help move humanity forward in ways you probably don't even realize.

Never stop creating, and never let anyone or anything hold you back from being able to create.

HOW TO APPLY THIS

So we learned that guitar is divided primarily into 3 categories: Technique, Theory, and Creativity.

- Technique and Theory build through the Pinnacle/Foundation Theory sequence [Foundation - Encode - Pinnacle - New Foundation - Expand]
- Creativity is both a state and an expression of the development of Technique and Theory.
- The goal is to maximize your ability with Technique and Theory, and to access the greatest depths of Creativity.

Practice Hacker Tip: Create Synergy with the 3 Fundamental Aspects of Guitar to attain mastery.

THE SCIENCE OF LEARNING

Secret 4

—

Building the Bridge: The Development of Technique & Theory

There are certain triggers that are responsible for growth as a musician, and really in general. Understanding them allows us to primarily focus on them when we practice, increasing our results exponentially, while removing wasting time and effort.

We often try to learn or improve skills by using methods that don't properly trigger growth and therefore, we waste a lot of time, energy, and potential. In fact, without understanding how to improve our ability to learn and grow, we waste money on lessons, resources, books, and courses. Knowledge is as good as our ability to use it.

We're always told to practice more. If we just practice more, we'll get better, right? Classic tenant of the Old Framework. People mean well when they say this, but they don't really understand what it means. When I first started guitar, that's what I did. I played all day and night. I thought that to make more progress on guitar, I simply needed more time in a day to practice. But I hit limits pretty quickly, and when life began to pile on responsibility and limit my 'free time,' I started to lose my abilities and remained stuck for many years.

This was a massive point of stress for me and it ate away at every fibre of my being. I'm sure you can relate to that feeling. Feeling like everyone else is talented, but you've hit your limit. Or that if you only had more time, you could be as good as them. Or maybe they just got lucky. Or you're just too busy working - you don't have time for guitar. Think about how many people give up music because it's 'too hard.' This isn't because music is hard, it's mostly because they don't know how to learn in a way that speeds up the process, therefore, they waste time, energy, potential, and even money by practicing ineffectively.

The Fundamentals of Skill Building help outline how skills are developed: the sequence to learn in, building Foundations, Encoding, creating Pinnacles, and developing new Foundations. To enhance this process, it's necessary to Make the Pinnacle of Others Your Foundation. However, I wanted to know what was actually responsible for this progress - the actual mechanism at play. I felt like something was still missing.

With fitness, we know we should go to the gym and work out. Many go to the gym and do random exercises, don't really control their diet, and have no plan - then wonder why they don't get the results they want. Compare that to people who follow a system or routine that's designed intentionally to engage you with the mechanisms responsible for growth. The difference? The framework.

In seeking to create elite results, we need an elite framework - so I knew that there had to be a similar set of mechanisms that created elite results for guitarists.

Through my research, I came across a couple of the main factors responsible for learning and development: **Neurogenesis** and **Neuroplasticity**. However, it wasn't until I heard about **Myelinogenesis** from Joshua Voiles that it completed the understanding for me. Thank you Josh for bringing it to my attention - it's a key element.

Focusing on these 3 areas will create the results we desire. That's what's important. There are likely many other processes at play but we don't want to lose the forest for the trees.

NEURAL PATHWAYS [The Bridge]

- **What it is:** it's the connection or pathway between Neurons [key parts of the nervous system]
- **What it's like:** a road between two cities - what traffic travels on while moving between them.
- These are either being created [Neurogenesis], being changed/modified [Neuroplasticity] or being strengthened/enhanced to improve connectivity and speed [Myelinogenesis].

Neural Pathways are the connections between Neurons. Neurogenesis is the creation of new Neural Pathways.

#1 NEUROGENESIS [Building the Bridge]

- **What it is:** the creation of new Neural Pathways.
- **What it's like:** the creation of the road between two cities, allowing traffic to travel between them.
- This happens when you're learning something new - you're creating new Neurons. Also, your depth of learning directly correlates to the intensity of the experience, also known as emotion. The greater the emotion associated with your learning, the stronger the memory formed and therefore, retention and recall.

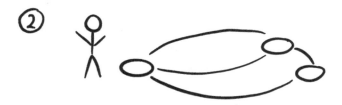

Neuroplasticity is the changing or modification of existing Neural Pathways.

#2 NEUROPLASTICITY [Modifying the Bridge]

- **What it is:** changing or modifying existing Neural Pathways.
- **What it's like:** connecting a city to multiple cities with new roads or fixing/changing old roads to connect cities - maybe even improving them or rebuilding them.
- This happens when you're connecting something newly learned with things you already know. This helps greatly enhance learning, as it develops the knowledge across multiple dimensions.
- Just like Neurogenesis, your depth of learning directly correlates to the intensity of the experience, also known as emotion. The greater the emotion associated with your learning, the stronger the memory formed and therefore, retention and recall.

Myelinogenesis is the strengthening of existing Neural Pathways, making communication faster, and deepening integration and automation

#3 MYELINOGENESIS [Strengthening the Bridge]

- **What it is:** strengthening existing Neural Pathways - improving connection/speed of information transfer.
- **What it's like:** like adding more lanes to the roads between cities, making them able to support more traffic, or increasing the speed limit/efficiency of travel.
- This happens primarily through perfected repetition that Encodes patterns, internalizing them, and pushes adaptation - establishing higher Foundations.

HOW TO APPLY THIS

When learning, we want to focus on maximizing our ability to learn. In other words, we want to improve the learning process by being aware of the mechanisms at play. We want to focus on and optimize our practice around them. This is the core of The Elite Framework and of the Practice Hacker's approach to practice. This is why traditional practice methods [the Old Framework] are ineffective and don't produce results. They are always focused on *what* you're learning, not *how* you're learning.

One of the best ways to enhance your depth of learning is by developing a strong emotional connection or response to what you're learning. This helps improve memory retention and recall.

Through perfected repetition [Encoding] you integrate and automate what you're learning at each level which allows you to push beyond adaptation; developing Pinnacles and New Foundations.

Now we understand the process of skill development: Pinnacle/Foundation Theory and what makes it work: Neurogenesis, Neuroplasticity, and Myelinogenesis. It's simply a matter of how you engage with them.

Now that awareness has removed mystery, the path can truly begin.

Practice Hacker Tip: By pushing our comfort zone as we're learning and Encoding, we cultivate high-intensity emotional states that enhance the depth of learning across all dimensions. Get uncomfortable. Push. Progress.

Secret 5

Synergy & Expansion: The Development of Creativity

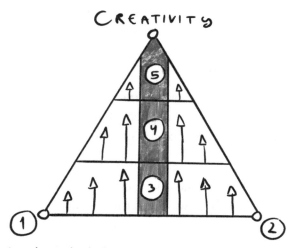

There are 5 main pathways that build Creativity: [1] Technique, [2] Theory, [3] Health, [4] Inspiration, and your [5] Ideal State.

Growing up in a creative household had a lot of benefits. From a young age, I explored Creativity in many ways - specifically music and guitar. However, like most people, I was never really aware of what made it work. I was never really in control of my state. I was reactionary. Some days I would be flowing with ideas and other days there was nothing - absolutely nothing. My states would fluctuate so much. I just thought that's how Creativity was. I'm sure you've felt this way too.

It wasn't until around high-school, or shortly after, that I started to really struggle with Creativity. I was detached from the process of developing and cultivating it. As a result, my ideas started feeling limited and outdated - even stale. I didn't feel inspired. I didn't feel motivated. I lacked creative vision. I was still operating from the Old Framework. I was stuck.

One thing I've learned is that change is the only constant and I wasn't changing. In fact, I was starting to go backwards. My skills began unravelling before my eyes. I started to believe that my best ideas were ones that I had years prior. I thought I had reached my peak and that it was downhill from there. What's terrible is that because of this, I wasn't releasing music. I was holding onto the music I did have because I felt like it was my best work and that nothing better would come. Talk about making a bad situation worse. How can I impact anyone with my music if I'm refusing to release it?

I always thought Creativity was some magical experience that just 'happened' when all the stars aligned. Like some mystical, spiritual happening. I wasn't aware that I could intentionally cultivate it or develop it. For me, it was fleeting.

It's funny, it wasn't until I started diving deeper into personal development that I realized that Creativity was something you could actually develop. Many people in that space are entrepreneurs and they are always looking for ways to maximize Creativity to develop new ideas, better run their businesses, and increase their own productivity and ultimately their quality of life.

As I dove deeper into this world, it opened me up to understanding Creativity in a much different light. It's a state. And any state is a result of the relationship between your mind and your body.

No wonder I struggled with this. For many years I was taking terrible care of my health. I would eat fast food all the time. I rarely drank water. I wasn't working out. I would play video games all night. I would sleep all day. I wasn't educating or improving myself. I was reactionary to the world around me, and my Creativity reflected that. The chaos of the external world was becoming the chaos of my internal world.

If I wanted to improve my Creativity, I had to begin to change what was responsible for my state: my mind and my body.

#1/2 TECHNIQUE & THEORY

Creativity is a higher expression of the ability and understanding you have with Technique and Theory, as well as the Synergy between them. Creativity is also an inspired or cultivated state; something you can access, express, and understand through the use of Technique and Theory.

Our goal here is to be able to fully express, without limitation, whatever our creative vision is. Which means our tools of expression [Technique and Theory] should continue to be developed. They are the Foundation in which Creativity is able to blossom.

Think of a painter. The greater their ability and understanding of Technique and Theory, the greater their awareness of what's possible. This awareness can open up new creative ideas unavailable to most people. They are able to give the painting whatever is needed to fully express their vision. They don't need to think about the Technique and Theory they are using - they simply use it. They are operating from highly developed sets of Pinnacles and Foundations; each brushstroke, each layer, each blend of colours, each application of contrast and depth is automatic and is able to serve its purpose.

They are one with the painting. They are the painting, and they use what's needed to cultivate their creative vision. Nothing more. Nothing less. This is mastery.

As guitarists, as musicians, as artists - this is our ultimate goal; to be uninhibited in expressing whatever we choose through our given medium [in this case, guitar]. Therefore, we want to maximize both Technique and Theory. Everything we learn and work on should have a creative application. We should always be raising our Foundation.

#3 HEALTH

I like to think of the human body/mind as a modem. We transmit signals and also receive them. What the internet is to the modem, Creativity is to us. The better the hardware, materials, and wiring, the greater the connection, function, and speed we have to the internet. In my opinion, the same goes for Creativity.

Therefore, we want to ensure all of our parts are functioning as optimally as possible. We want to be able to transmit and receive the highest quality signals [Creativity] with the greatest of ease. We also want to focus on being in the states that produce or explore the highest quality signals [Creativity] as often as we can, not limited by our hardware, materials, or wiring.

In this case, we need to address the health of our bodies and minds as they are the hardware, materials, and wiring that will maximize our Creativity.

I'm not a dietician or a registered healthcare professional. I'm only sharing with you some information I've researched and personally tested in the pursuit of maximizing health and Creativity. Do your own research, consult with your physician, and make informed decisions for yourself.

DIET

Diet is a strange thing. You'd think that as humans, we'd all have a single way of eating that worked for everyone, but that isn't the case. Everyone is a bit different. However, in my opinion you want to focus your diet on nutrition that improves cognitive function, reduces inflammation, provides long-lasting energy, and is easily digested. You also want to remove foods that have anti-nutrients [Oxalates, Phytates, etc.] and that are unnatural. Our bodies are great at adapting, but also replace cells based on the nutrients you feed it [or don't feed it]. Therefore, the better you eat, the better your mind and body will function, even into old age.

This is described a bit later on in more detail but essentially stick with natural foods and remove or restrict processed foods and sugars. Ensure you're getting enough saturated fat/cholesterol for hormone regulation and cell development. Get enough vitamin B12 and D3. Drink enough water. Don't combine foods that inhibit proper absorption or digestion of nutrients [fats & carbs together, anti-nutrients, etc.].

Just become aware of the foods you eat and how they make you feel. Are they boosting your energy? Can you focus better or is your brain foggy? Do your joints ache? Is your memory suffering? Do you feel bloated? Do you feel better eating more fat and protein? Or do you feel better eating more carbs?

EXERCISE

Cardio, strength training, stretching, movement. The goal is to improve and increase blood flow, develop strength and muscle, and improve heart health [ability and recovery]. Heart health especially helps with getting into a flow-state and deeper levels of relaxation. By exercising and taking care of your body, you're not only increasing your ability to enter creative states, but also improving your overall quality of life.

MORNING/EVENING ROUTINES

We all have routines, but most times we are unaware of them. Do your routines serve you? Are you being reactive or proactive? Do you wake up in the morning right before you need to be at school/work, barely getting yourself together, and rushing out the door to get there on time? Or do you take a few minutes in the morning for yourself to read, to meditate, to work on a project - all putting you in a great mental state for the rest of the day? Many people fall into the first category and unfortunately those people, as well as those around them, suffer greatly as a result.

By spending some time each morning getting yourself into an Ideal State, working on a project or Goal, or focusing on something that builds you up, you're setting yourself up for success. No matter what else happens that day, you've accomplished something for you, and for your future! By improving yourself and becoming more, you're able to serve those around you to a much greater degree. Total 360 win. Same thing with nighttime. Do you wind down before bed? Reflect on the day, read, relax? Or do you just watch TV, go on social media, play video games, have a few drinks, stay up late, and then eventually go to sleep?

As you'd imagine, one is going to set you up to be in control of your state [proactive], and the other is going cause you to be a product of the world around you [reactive]. If you truly want to accomplish anything in life, it starts with controlling your state. The best way, in my opinion, to do this is through a morning/evening routine.

By creating a routine that empowers you to be in a more resourceful, controlled state, you're setting yourself up for success. You'll be able to accomplish your goals with much greater ease. Plus the gratification and excitement you'll feel when you're accomplishing something that's important to you is an incredible catalyst for Creativity. Seek to be proactive, not reactive! Control your state, control your life.

MIND

After graduating from high-school or university, many people stop learning unless their jobs require it. We spend our whole lives up until that point growing, learning, and evolving [albeit, not in an effective way]. We are designed for growth. It's imprinted in us. Yet most people stop learning. And if you're not growing, you're dying.

If the world is changing around you and you aren't, you're going to fall behind. You're going to lack new ideas. You're not going to be inspired. You're going to be limited. You won't be able to compete. You won't be able to grow. Your brain is a supercomputer, but if it sits there collecting dust for years, by the time you need to use it it's going to need so many upgrades and updates that it might not even work.

This might seem a bit dramatic, but you get the point. Continue to educate yourself, grow your mind and create new connections. Read books, take courses, find mentors - just keep learning. Follow your passions and interests in a way that's constructive and builds toward the life you truly want to live. By developing this Habit, you'll soon crave the process of improving yourself. It isn't a chore. It opens up your mind, and therefore your Creativity. You'll gain new ideas, new Inspirations, new perceptions, and a greater depth in which you can explore them. In fact, you'll gain a greater depth in which you can explore life.

#4 INSPIRATION

Inspiration is the gateway for Creativity. It's the switch that allows for the floodgates to open. There are many ways to access Inspiration.

Entering Inspiration

- Watch a movie or play a video game that has inspiring music, stories, characters, or imagery.

  - How does it make you feel? What experience does it create?

- Create a list of songs, riffs, or ideas that inspire you.

  - What makes them inspire you? Is it the emotion of the scale/modes, the catchiness of the hook, the groove and movement of the rhythms?

  - Try taking parts of what inspires you and apply it to your own music. Maybe it's using the same chords and modifying the rhythm. Maybe it's exploring a similar type of melody.

- • Whatever you do, aim to evoke a similar emotion or feeling as you were inspired by. You're adding to your toolkit, creating similar experiences in the future.

- ■ Look for Inspiration in unlikely places.

  - • Plays, nature, books, other genres of music, environments, colours or textures, memories, ideas, themes, stories, hopes or dreams, nightmares or struggles.

  - • You can find Inspiration in everything - look at life like a child, you'll be surprised at how inspired even the wind can make you if you have an open mind.

- ■ Try taking emotions you feel, whether 'good' or 'bad,' and capture them in a riff or a song.

  - • See what you come up with. Use music as your journal.

- ■ Test yourself.

  - • Even if it's not something you're currently learning, pick a random scale, chord, chord progression, or pattern. Use that and try to write something new.

- ■ Just start.

  - • Just try to write 3 notes. Most times you'll do that and then you'll hear the 4th note, then you'll find a few more and then a few more. Next thing you know; you've been writing for an hour. Just start somewhere. Start small. But start!

Transforming Uninspired States

- ■ With all of these inspired states, what does your mental imagery look like? Bright, colourful, loud, moving, etc.? Close your eyes and experience it.

- How does your body feel? Are you breathing differently? Is your chest puffed up more? Are you standing up straighter with your shoulders back? Are you smiling?

- How are you talking or thinking, is it more rhythmic, more excited, more dynamic?

- Take note of these things when you're entering states of Inspiration. Then when you want to access Inspiration, try emulating the qualities you've recognized within that state. Be as accurate as possible. This can help you understand yourself better and you'll more easily be able to enter states of Inspiration and Creativity without needing external factors.

- External factors simply influence our internal state by how we respond to it. The goal is to control our responses, to control our state. It's about being proactive, not reactive.

#5 IDEAL STATE

One of the best ways for accessing Creativity is through achieving an Ideal State. We will be discussing this more in depth in **Secret 16**.

Some examples:

- Meditation/Prayer
- Mindfulness
- Affirmations
- Visualization
- Ritual/Routine/Habit
- Anchors

Our goal with Creativity is to access it at will without being limited by ourselves. So being aware of what inspires you allows you to use it to cultivate the creative states you need.

HOW TO APPLY THIS

Creativity stems from the level of development and Synergy of Technique and Theory. Creativity is also a state which we can access and explore. Like being a modem, Creativity is the internet.

We should look in different areas of music, art, film, or anything that could potentially inspire a creative state. We should become more and more aware of the particular triggers we have as individuals to inspire Creativity. Once we can identify them, we can actively engage with them - sparking Creativity and Inspiration independent of uncontrolled factors. We become proactive. We control our state.

> **Practice Hacker Tip:** Master your tools [Technique and Theory]. Master your state. Become the painting.

Secret 6

Knowledge/Integration Framework

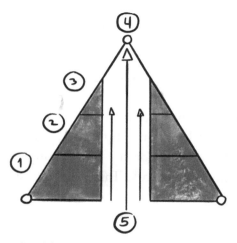

The Learning Process has 4 distinct phases: [1] Knowledge, [2] Isolation, [3] Application, [4] Integration. However, there is a [5] Master Approach that pushes right through from Knowledge to Integration - quickly

Pinnacle/Foundation Theory opened up my perception of how skills were developed. It was a truly massive transformation. Establishing the Foundation, Encoding, building Pinnacles, and creating New Foundations. So simple, yet so powerful. But even with that, I still felt something was missing. Were there different levels to the Integration process? Were there levels to developing and using Technique and Theory? Was there a certain sequence or a way to speed this process up? I still had questions. I felt like I had the key but it was just missing a single piece for it to unlock the door to my musical potential.

Have you ever tried to learn a new scale or bit of Theory but had no idea how to use it in a musical context? Or maybe you learned a new pattern or exercise but you were stuck using those notes, in that order? The reason for this is because you're not taking what you've learned [Knowledge] and fully internalizing it and its applications [Integration]. Honestly, this happens to most guitarists. It's certainly happened to me.

As per the Old Framework, they say you just need more time. You just need to practice more. Then you'll get it, eventually you'll integrate it. Just put in more time. Yet, has anyone considered that the reason this process normally takes so long, is because people are fundamentally practicing wrong?

On my journey to discover the missing piece, I came across some of Tom Hess' work. He is a world-renowned guitar teacher, and a brilliant mind when it comes to the world of guitar. He vividly identified 3 levels of guitar practice: Isolation, Application, and Integration. I took that information and expanded on it a bit, creating what I now call the Knowledge/Integration Framework. This was the missing piece.

KNOWLEDGE

- The base knowledge/understanding of what you're wanting to learn.
- Example: learning a new Technique - how to move your hands and the base motor skill function required.

ISOLATION

- Work on it outside of a musical context.
- Example: working on an exercise that uses the new Technique - creating and Encoding new connections.

APPLICATION

- Work on it within a musical context.

- Example: using the Technique with a certain scale or mode, perhaps even adding rhythmic variance.

INTEGRATION

- Combine it with other musical skills.

- Example: practice one Technique with many different concepts, practice one concept with many different Techniques.

MASTER APPROACH

You might look at the above and think that it's a lot of linear work to do to create your desired result. If you were to work step-by-step in that sequence, then you'd be correct. However, there is an approach that speeds up this process greatly. It implements the Building the Bridge framework [as we discussed in **Secret 4**], and also engages all of the Pillars of Practicology [which we will discuss in **Secret 9**]. This Master Approach is:

CREATING!

True understanding comes from application and experience. You can also view this as wisdom. To know something is to be able to teach it. And there is no better way to do this than through creating with it.

When you write music, you usually create something from the heart that excites and breathes life into you. This creates a powerful emotional response, which as we know, is very important for memory formation, retention, and recall. It enhances the depth of learning.

When you write with something new, you're automatically applying it in a musical context, and you're applying it to other concepts you know. This further enhances memory formation, retention, and recall; this is the quickest pathway to Integration. This is the Master Approach.

So simple, yet so profound. You'll learn even more about this and how it affects the Pillars of Practicology in **Secret 9.**

HOW TO APPLY THIS

To effectively learn something, move it through the Knowledge/Integration Framework.

- Knowledge
- Isolation
- Application
- Integration

The quickest way to do this is through the Master Approach: creating. This uses the Technique and Theory you're learning, combining it with the Technique and Theory you know. It utilizes your Creativity as an expression of Technique and Theory, as well as a state. It enhances your depth of learning by cultivating a greater emotional response, and it further enhances the use and application of the Pillars of Practicology [which we will discuss in **Secret 9**].

Practice Hacker Tip: Hack the Knowledge/Integration process through utilizing the Master Approach. Create!

PRACTICE STRATEGIES

Secret 7

Performance Measurements

When seeking perfection there are 3 types of Performance Measurements to consider: [1]
Musical, [2] Technical, [3] Repetition.

I remember years ago when I first picked up the guitar I would play all
day and night, however I never really knew what I was doing. I didn't
know if something was correct or incorrect. I didn't know what the right
rhythms felt like. I couldn't identify pitches. I didn't know if I was holding
the pick properly. I didn't even know if the guitar was in tune. I didn't
know what I didn't know - but at least I was having fun. I was a guitarist.

As with anything new, I initially made some progress in the early stages. I was Encoding patterns and movements which became my Foundation. However, they were incorrect. Once the 'beginner gains' wore off, I was left with an incomplete and faulty Foundation that felt like it was ready to collapse at any time. If you aren't Encoding perfected movements, you cannot scale to higher speeds and greater applications. If your Foundation isn't perfectly constructed, any structure you build will fall. This becomes the demise of so many guitarists, and was almost mine.

Because of not understanding this process, I got stuck for a long time. Most people just tell you to 'practice more' [Old Framework], but again, most people aren't aware of how to actually practice or how to build skills. They just repeat the same things over and over again until they eventually figure out how to do it better. It's such an inefficient process. After countless hours of incorrect practice, there's enough correct practice that compounds to create a result. Because of this, this affirms the notion that you just need to 'practice more' to get better, which continues pushing the same lie that destroys countless guitarist's hopes, dreams, and careers.

The core of Practice Secrets of the Pros is The Elite Framework. The core of The Elite Framework is to quickly identify issues and fix them by properly Encoding perfected patterns so we can build them up to where we need them. We can't do this if we don't know what 'perfect' is. That's where **Performance Measurements** come into play. They become our guiding pillars for building towards greater perfection.

This took me years to realize. I received the odd lesson but I was mostly self-taught. Through a lot of trial and error - as well as comparing my playing to the different tapes, CDs, and other resources I was learning from, I developed a greater ability to self-regulate. I finally understood what I needed to look out for. I had a better understanding of Performance Measurements - now I could perfect them. I wish I had learned these things early on, but at least now I could use them to correct past mistakes and carve out a new future for myself. A future free of limitation. A strong

Foundation building into Pinnacles and into even stronger Foundations - ever expanding.

Guitar practice will require you to become better at listening and understanding what's correct and incorrect. Most traditional guitar lessons can be a waste of time because of using the Old Framework, however, if you're brand new to guitar, I recommend at least a few basic lessons. This is because you lack the ability to properly self-regulate and it's difficult to teach yourself the nuances of self-regulation. Teaching yourself the basics through online material isn't impossible, but I still recommend at least a few in-person lessons to help you get started with developing your Foundation quicker. This is a part of Making the Pinnacle of Others Your Foundation. There's no need to suffer for the sake of being 'self-taught.' Do what's necessary for your growth and for your path. Do not get in the way of your own success.

To truly use The Elite Framework to its fullest potential, you need to be a master of self-regulation and a master of Performance Measurements.

MUSICAL

Musical Measurements have to do with the musical elements of playing and practice. This is what will allow you to correctly learn and play the notes - mastering their qualities and their rhythms.

- Correct Notes and Pitches

    - This is where you're ensuring that you're playing the right Notes, Pitches, Melodies, and Chords. Without this, you can't do anything else.

- Rhythms

    - Rhythm is critical to music. It's the organization of weak and strong elements to create movement. Without Rhythm, music can't flow - it can't move. Therefore, you must ensure you're playing the correct Rhythms and staying in time.

- Tempo

  - The speed or rate the piece is played at. This is usually the target you will be seeking to hit using correct Performance Measurements. We want to do what's correct, Encode it, and bring it up to the desired Tempo. This is often represented as BPM [Beats Per Minute].

- Articulations

  - Articulations determine how a single note or event sounds - the quality. This can relate to its attack, decay, and timbre, but it all has to do with the tonal quality of the note/event. Though this is more nuanced, it is incredibly important.

  - Anyone can play the same note - but not everyone plays a note the same way. As they say: tone is in the fingers. This is where that saying comes from - the particular Articulation you give the note/event to create the desired effect/expression of emotion. Therefore, you must Encode the correct Articulations so they become automatic parts of your playing.

  - The most common Articulations for guitarists are Staccato and Legato [including Hammer-Ons, Pull-Offs, and Slides]

- Dynamics

  - This refers to the contrast, variation, and relationship between the volume of notes or parts of a piece, more specifically: loudness and softness. This is another more nuanced element of guitar, but is critical in creating emotion and expression.

In this context, the Correct Notes, Pitches, Rhythms, and Tempo would establish your initial Foundation. Once those are Encoded and internalized, you would express them with more depth through Articulations and Dynamics.

TECHNICAL

Technical Measurements have more to do with the control, precision, and cleanliness of your playing.

- Efficiency of Motion

    - The focus here is to move your picking hand as little as possible while having maximum impact and control.

    - You should have no tension in your hand, wrist, elbow, forearm, shoulder, or back. Everything should flow and be smooth. It should be efficient.

- Fluidity of Motion

    - Focus on fretting as light as possible, with as little movement or stress between changing notes, without sacrificing note quality.

- Pick Mastery

    - The pick should have minimal obstruction. Efficiency of Motion should fix a lot of issues, but furthermore, you want to use as little of the pick as possible to get the desired effect and control. Consider techniques such as pickslanting to further optimize this. Troy Grady and Ben Eller have great content on this very topic.

    - Become pick-aware. Slow down what you're playing enough to not sacrifice how you'd actually play it at full speed and watch what your pick is doing as you're playing the piece.

- Is it clashing with other strings? Is it scraping? Is it hopping too much? Is it getting caught? Is your hand tensing up? Do you need to adjust the angle or the motion? Do you need to start on an upstroke instead of down stroke for a particular part?

- Precision and Cleanliness

  - One of the most important parts of playing guitar is playing clean; minimizing string noise, excessive scraping, unnecessary pick noise, and undesired ringing out.

Each Musical Measurement should be Encoded with these Technical Measurements.

If you want to see the ideal example of perfected Performance Measurements, check out Rick Graham. He is one of the most efficient guitarists I've ever seen, alongside Guthrie Govan. If you want more information on Pick Mastery, Troy Grady has an entire series where he breaks down picking secrets from top-level shredders.

REPETITION

Our goal is to properly Encode patterns, pieces, and basically anything we're learning or working on. This happens at multiple levels. We identify mistakes, correct them, and Encode them at the Meta [song] level, Macro [section] level, Micro [measure] level, and Nano [note] level as explained in the Pathway to Completion Sequence in **Secret 17**. More on that later, but for now, just understand that when seeking to learn and practice something correctly, these are the different levels of its application that we will need to ensure we're Encoding.

- Repeat a section
- Repeat a measure
- Repeat a group of notes

- Play from the beginning

MASTER STRATEGY

Our Foundation will first start with the Musical Measurements of Correct Notes, Pitches, and Rhythms.

Using Tempo as our goal, we will Encode perfected Musical Measurements alongside perfected Technical Measurements through multiple levels of Repetition. The process to do this will be explained in far greater detail in The Elite Framework.

Once internalized, we then focus on building the more nuanced, higher-expression Measurements, such as Articulations and Dynamics, because we now have the Foundation established to support them.

SIMPLIFY THE PROCESS

One thing to keep in mind is that everyone learns a bit differently. There is no one-size-fits-all approach to guitar practice. Some people might find it easier to build correct Notes, Pitches, Rhythms, Articulations, and Dynamics all at once. Some might find a different order that makes sense for them.

The point of this chapter is simply to outline the different Performance Measurements that you will need to build towards perfection, and how to approach them using Pinnacle/Foundation Theory.

We often get so caught up in the details that it holds us back from building the Foundation to support real progress. This approach simplifies that by focusing on the basic aspects of what you're learning first, Encoding them to become internalized and automatic, then exploring higher and higher applications; building into greater Pinnacles and even greater Foundations.

Use this information in whatever way best suits your needs.

GUITAR PRACTICE... AND BABIES?

Newborn babies are born with very little motor skill function. They can't really use their arms and legs in any meaningful way. If you were to try to teach them the nuances of elite-level soccer skills, or advanced acrobatics, they wouldn't even be able to comprehend it. This is because their Foundation is not built to that level.

But through the process of skill building [identifying mistakes, correcting them, and Encoding them], they eventually start to use their limbs. First, they crawl, then they walk, then they run. Next thing you know, they are doing incredible feats beyond what even you are capable of doing.

When they are performing or learning incredible feats, do you think they are hyper-aware and focused on building the ability to crawl or walk, or how to make their hands move? No. This is because these motions have become internalized - they are automatic, they are default, they are Encoded. They have become Pinnacles, which have become higher Foundations on which they are building new Pinnacles.

It's the same thing for guitar. The more you master this process, the higher your Foundations become. The higher your Foundations become, the more you can focus on higher applications; building new Pinnacles and even greater Foundations. Each level you Encode and build becomes internalized and automatic, leaving you able to explore greater applications without needing to focus on the basics.

See why it's so critical to understand the processes at work so you can focus your practice, and ultimately your guitar pathways on them? See why it's so important to make sure your Foundation is properly established?

What makes the world's best guitarist's so good? There is the obvious element of Creativity and the emotional quality of their music, but we consider them great because of their mastery of Musical and Technical Measurements. They play perfectly. They have incredible Technique and proficiency. They have complete command over their instruments. They are the painting.

HOW TO APPLY THIS

The primary goal for guitar is efficiency. Efficiency is what allows you to scale speed and precision. Maximum impact, minimum force. Maximum output, minimum input.

When addressing any part, pay attention to these Performance Measurements. When you encounter an issue, refer to these Performance Measurements. When aiming to have something 'perfect', pay attention to these Performance Measurements. You will then use The Elite Framework to fix and work through them. Before you can self-regulate, you need to understand what you're self-regulating. In the next chapter, we'll go over how to apply these Performance Measurements and how to improve your ability to self-regulate your practice and progress.

> **Practice Hacker Tip:** The pathway to mastery is travelled by Encoding and building higher Foundations through perfected Performance Measurements.

Secret 8

Self-Regulation & Performance Evaluation

Individual music practice is a form of self-regulated learning.

Lack of progress on guitar, in music, or really any area of life, is often the result of ignorance. You aren't always aware of your issues. You aren't always aware of how to fix them. You don't know what you don't know - this was certainly the case in my own life. I was operating from the Old Framework. It took me a long time to identify issues, which means it took me a long time to fix them. This simply reinforced the false, Limiting Belief that I needed to practice more to get better. That I just needed *more time*.

The reason many people never progress beyond their current state is because they aren't aware that they need to change, or even know *how* to change. As a result they stay at the same level for years - sometimes even their entire lives, thinking they have reached their Limit. They believe they just aren't talented enough or that guitar or music just isn't for them. This simply isn't true - they just need the right system; the right framework. The core of this is understanding Self-Regulation.

As I mentioned before, this is a benefit of having a teacher or mentor in the early stages of learning; Making the Pinnacle of Others Your Foundation.

Even though I had developed my understanding of Performance Measurements intuitively through years of trial and error, I was still very unaware of the process of Self-Regulation. Because of my own lack of awareness, it greatly limited my ability to improve on guitar until at one point everything came to a screeching halt. I wasn't Encoding patterns correctly or efficiently, in fact I was actually internalizing a lot of destructive and limiting habits. I wasn't establishing Foundations or building Pinnacles in the right way. As a result, I thought I had reached my Limit, that I wasn't talented enough, and that maybe guitar and music just weren't for me.

This sparked my obsession with uncovering the truth behind guitar practice and skill development - it was the catalyst that initiated my search for answers.

I dove deep into the best scientific literature and information I could find on music practice and Self-Regulation. One of those studies was called *Self-regulating Learning Strategies in Instrumental Music Practice* [Nielsen 2001]. Though it outlines a lot of great information, the basic premise is simple: advanced students demonstrate more skillful self-regulated learning. In other words, the better you can self-regulate, the better musician you will become.

Music practice is a form of self-regulated learning. You're likely not going to have a teacher with you 24/7, so you need to master your ability to self-regulate if you want to become the guitarist you've always dreamed of being. You need to quickly become aware of issues as they arise so you can fix them and continue building towards perfection. The quicker you can do this, the quicker you can attain mastery. This is where Self-Regulation and Performance Evaluation come into play.

PROCESS OF SELF-REGULATION

- Set a Goal
- Have multiple strategies to pull from
- Progress towards the Goal
- Identify issues
- Work on the issues [choosing the best/most applicable strategy]
- Evaluate Performance
- Repeat

METHODS FOR PERFORMANCE EVALUATION

#1 RECORD YOURSELF ON VIDEO

- Allows you to observe issues with the different Performance Measurements.
- Allows you to more effectively compare with the source material [audio or video].
- Allows you to share with friends or other musicians who can properly critique you [forums, online groups, hangouts, etc.].

#2 SELF-ANALYSIS

- Allows you to understand what feels right or wrong as you're playing - correcting as needed.

- This will be developed through the other Performance Evaluation methods as well.

#3 LESSONS

- Allows real-time person-to-person feedback to address issues.
- Ideal for beginners, though anyone can benefit from the wisdom of a master.

HOW TO APPLY THIS

To quicken the pathway to mastery, one must be able to instantly identify inconsistencies or mistakes, test them against the standard or ideal, and make adjustments to attain the desired outcome.

Your ability to self-regulate will ultimately decide what you're able to get out of guitar, and life. It will also decide what you're able to get out of this book. This book is based on gaining awareness, applying the principles, and then optimizing through Self-Regulation. Keep that in mind. Limited awareness limits results.

Find the best method for Performance Evaluation that allows you to identify problems quickly and correct them. At first this might be with the help and critique of others. Alternatively, you might just compare yourself against the source material. Whatever path you choose, a strategic, focused, and consistent approach is key.

As you progress, continue to explore how you prioritize and sequence strategies based on the Goals you have and note their outcomes. This is a key part of Tracking and Optimization, which we will discuss more in **Secret 18**, but ultimately just refine what works and discard what doesn't. The quicker you can do this, the quicker your pathway to mastery. Increase your awareness, increase your results.

Practice Hacker Tip: Your ability to self-regulate directly correlates with your ability to use and benefit from The Elite Framework. Master Self-Regulation and Performance Evaluation to truly Maximize Output and Minimize Input - becoming the guitarist you've always dreamed of being.

Secret 9

Pillars of Practicology

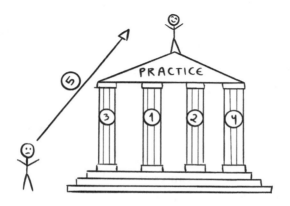

The 4 Pillars of Practicology build the Temple: [1] Mental, [2] Physical, [3] Aural, [4] Kinaesthetic. However, the [5] Pillar Hack enhances this process.

When you think of guitar practice, what comes to mind? For most, it's picking up a guitar and sitting down with a metronome, working on different scales, chords, or patterns. For others, it's jamming to your favourite songs, improvising, or maybe even writing.

However, what do all of these have in common? They all start with the Physical practice of guitar.

When I was younger, I didn't have much perception of what guitar practice was, nevermind if there were different types of guitar practice. As I grew older though, I became more aware of my ability to hear and work on music in my head. I would often sit down and write a riff and then throughout the following days, the riff would play over and over again in my mind.

Sometimes, I would visualize myself playing it. Sometimes, if I had a recording of the riff, I'd listen to it over and over again. Sometimes, I would hum the riff and tap my foot to the beat. As a result, when I actually sat down with the guitar, I would be able to play the riff much better, and I'd often have new ideas to explore.

Have you ever experienced something like this? If so, then you've engaged with the Pillars of Practicology.

In short, the Pillars of Practicology are the core pillars that build your practice routine. To maximize the benefits of your practice, you need to engage all 4 pillars: Mental, Physical, Aural, and Kinaesthetic. However, there is a Pillar Hack that allows you to enhance this process and get even more out of your practice sessions. Similar to how the Master Approach accelerates you through the Knowledge/Integration Framework.

Like most people, I was unaware of these other types of practice. But now that we have awareness, we can consciously engage with the Pillars of Practicology to amplify our results and progress towards mastery.

On my journey to discover the Practice Secrets of the Pros, I came across many different resources and studies. One particular study, called *Effects of Mental Practice and Modeling on Guitar and Vocal Performance* [Theiler 1995] outlined the benefit of utilizing different types of practice, primarily noting that Physical and Mental practice in combination is more effective than Physical practice alone.

#1 MENTAL PRACTICE

Mental practice utilizes the mind. You might visualize the piece; the movements, the patterns, the notes, the structure, the transitions, etc. You might also play back the piece in your mind, without using the Aural reference.

Whatever the approach, focus especially on problem areas. Solving them in your mind will help you solve them in real life.

Kind of like how reading the questions for a test primes your brain for finding the answers in the study material. Or how looking at a map and seeing the terrain and potential routes allows you to physically navigate the area much easier.

You can utilize Mental practice before Physical practice to better establish your Foundation, as well as after to better strengthen it.

#2 PHYSICAL PRACTICE

Physical practice deals with physically learning and practicing the piece; the movements, the patterns, the notes, the structure, the transitions, etc.

Mental practice has many benefits, and if you're an advanced player it can often be a replacement for Physical practice. However, just like with sports or lifting weights, you need to engage the Physical to develop your ability. You can't grow muscles just by thinking about it.

Using The Elite Framework, Physical practice is where the bulk of your work will take place. This is where you engage the Skill Development Zone.

#3 AURAL PRACTICE

This is a perfect way to prime your brain before learning something new.

Listen to the piece multiple times to build familiarity with it. It allows you to map out the terrain and establish a general outline of the piece [the Foundation].

The quicker you can establish the Foundation prior to Physically working on it, the quicker you can build the piece to perfection.

One of the best ways to know you have the Foundation established is when you're able to run through the entire piece in your head without needing the Aural model for reference.

#4 KINAESTHETIC PRACTICE

This form of practice is less talked about but is a very common form that most people engage with, though often unaware of it.

Ever whistle while doing the dishes? Ever tap your foot while you're singing or playing something? These are all forms of Kinaesthetic practice. This type of practice refers to working on fingerings, tapping rhythms, humming melodies, and other types of movements/expressions outside of Physical practice.

If you're running material through your mind or listening to it, or even if you're Physically practicing it, consider involving other parts of your physiology to strengthen and enhance the connections you're forming. Every bit counts.

PILLARS OF PRACTICOLOGY

As you can see, to maximize your ability to learn and integrate information, it's important to engage all of the Pillars of Practicology: Mental, Physical, Aural, and Kinaesthetic.

Most of the time, we engage with these processes naturally and we aren't always aware that we're doing it. But now that we understand their importance, by engaging the Pillars of Practicology we are more effectively building, modifying, and strengthening connections. In other words, we are improving all areas of learning by engaging different forms of practice.

As a result, you will learn faster, build your skills quicker, perform at a higher level, enhance your precision, and improve your expression - all without needing more Physical practice. This means you can practice anytime, anywhere, improving your results greatly.

#5 PILLAR HACK

What's the best way to engage all of the Pillars of Practicology? You guessed it:

CREATING!

Creating music is an emotional experience. You're often creating something that has meaning to you - it comes from the heart. This emotional response enhances the depth of learning.

Additionally, when you pull away from creating, the piece often continues playing in your head. You hear it over and over, usually hearing new ideas that you didn't think of before. Or when you go back to play it, you find it's much easier to play. This is because you've enhanced and strengthened these connections outside of Physical practice using Mental practice.

Oftentimes, throughout your day, you'll find yourself tapping your foot to the rhythm, humming the melody, or playing air guitar; pretending you're picking or fretting the parts. This further enhances and strengthens these connections, using Kinaesthetic practice.

Maybe you've even recorded this new creation and you find yourself listening to it over and over again as you're doing other tasks or going about your day. This engages Aural practice - further enhancing and strengthening these connections.

See how the process of creation is a multi-dimensional approach to learning and development? As you're applying new Techniques and Theory by creating with them, you're speeding through the Knowledge/Integration Framework and engaging all of the Pillars of Practicology. Additionally, your depth of learning is greatly enhanced by your emotional connection to it. It's insane how powerful creating is.

OUT OF SIGHT, WITHIN MIND

If you're struggling to complete what you're writing, or stuck with what you're working on, if you walk away at the height of the experience, it's like leaving an open-ended question for your mind to answer. Your brain is a computer and needs problems to solve, so by walking away at the peak of struggle, your mind will operate in the background to solve the problem.

We often get in the way of our own minds, however it's usually when we're occupied doing something else that our brain seems to find the solution to our problems. Funny how that works. Consider engaging with a different task [chores, exercise, reading, etc.] to allow your brain to calculate the answers in the background. Even consider walking away at the peak of struggle before going to bed, you might just solve the problem in your sleep.

HOW TO APPLY THIS

As a primary strategy, consider the following:

- **Before Physical Practice:**
  - Prepare by using Mental and Aural practice.
  - This can help you pre-establish your Foundation, familiarizing yourself with the material before actually learning it. This makes Physical practice much easier.
  - Consider using Kinaesthetic practice while you do this, or throughout your day, to develop stronger connections.

- Physical Practice:
  - Using The Elite Framework, this is where most of your work will take place.

- This can also include Kinaesthetic practice.

- You're creating new connections, as well as modifying, changing, and strengthening previous connections.

■ **After Physical Practice:**

- Include Mental practice and/or Aural practice to reinforce the material you've learned.

- This develops a deeper and more detailed map of it; further internalizing and automating the information.

- Consider using Kinaesthetic practice while you do this, or throughout your day, to develop stronger connections.

Practice Hacker Tip: Use the Pillar Hack to easily utilize the Pillars of Practicology, blast through the Knowledge/Integration Framework and enhance your depth of learning across multiple dimensions.

Secret 10

Productivity and the Compounding Effect

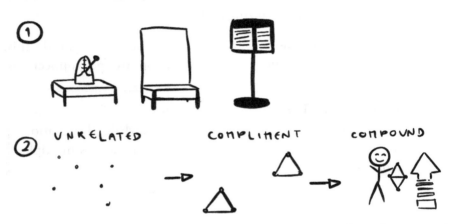

[1] Ensure you have a productive space dedicated to practice to reduce task-switching costs and distraction. [2] To compound your progress, work on complementary tasks/skills/Goals instead of unrelated ones.

Productivity requires freedom from distraction and limitation.

One of the biggest factors that has contributed to my ability to grow on guitar, and in life, is having a space that allows for the highest levels of Productivity. You don't want to have to reset your workspace every time you need to practice or work on something.

Remember, with Creativity we are looking to fully immerse ourselves in it, unhindered by limitation. An inefficient workspace is a massive limitation. Nothing kills Creativity more than process, procedure, and distraction. The same applies to practice and Productivity.

By having a dedicated space for practice; an area of your room, home, or somewhere else - you'll establish a connection between that space and Productivity. Through repeated use, you'll program your mind to access Productivity quicker, as well as increase the depth in which you can explore it.

As you can see, a productive space is critical to your success. However, to take your Productivity to the next level, you'll also want to engage what I call the Compounding Effect.

Years ago, when everything felt like it was falling apart in my life, it was the catalyst I needed to push forward. It provided me clarity and awareness, along with the drive I needed to take control of my destiny. A part of this clarity and awareness was the realization that I had many aspects of my life that I wasn't actively engaging with. In fact, many of them I was ignoring. No wonder I was in the position I was in.

As I began to walk this new path, I felt that I had to make up for lost time.

I looked to my idols and mentors and saw a common theme: they are all constantly improving their lives. They are always becoming more. So I knew if I wanted to make my dreams come true, if I wanted to take control of my destiny, I needed to follow their example; I needed to become more.

To do this, I started to fill my day up with morning routines, reading, courses, work, fitness, music, guitar, relationships, friends, family, and more. I would try to do 30 minutes of this, 60 minutes of that - yet I never felt like I was actually making progress. By the time I was into one task, I had to stop to do another. My day was completely full, stress was high, and I wasn't getting any results.

I remember after my first year of trying to set and accomplish Goals - I didn't complete any of them. Talk about a slap in the face. Imagine that. Your whole life is falling apart and you get this glimmer of hope. There's finally a chance - a light at the end of the tunnel. Then you hustle as hard as you can, getting up at 4:00am every day and working tirelessly so you can make things happen. Then, nothing. You didn't accomplish anything. You're no further ahead than you were before. In fact, you feel further behind.

Doubts began flooding my mind. Was I just not good enough to make progress in these areas? Could I not change or improve myself? Was I stuck like this forever? All of the sacrifice, all of the hard work, pushing myself in every way I could - yet I wasn't going anywhere. Why was I doing all of this? I had to be doing something wrong.

During this time, I was reading one of Tim Ferriss' books *The 4-Hour Workweek* and the answer to my problems revealed itself. Tim is known for many things, but one particular quality that stands out is his ability to maximize output while minimizing input. In his book, he outlines one of the main methods he uses to accomplish this: Chunking.

What is Chunking? Well first, let me explain the cost of task-switching. When we are doing a task, it can take anywhere up to 45 minutes to get into the groove or flow of it, where we're really locked in and enter a state of Productivity. Though there are methods to improve this, which we will discuss in **Secret 16**, it's no wonder I wasn't making progress towards my Goals. If I was only doing a task for 30-60 minutes, I would barely have enough time to enter a state of Productivity before I had to switch to the next task. As a result, I was always busy, but never productive. Being busy simply gave me the illusion of Productivity.

The Goal when engaging with a task is to enter a state of Productivity. If you interrupt it with other tasks, social media, an unproductive environment, or other distractions - you're pulling yourself out of that state. This is where Chunking comes into play. Combine similar tasks together in the same window of time so the cost of task-switching is minimal. So simple yet so powerful.

This is further optimized through the 80/20 Rule [also known as the Pareto Principle], which we will discuss in **Secret 13**. The idea is simple:

focus on the few tasks that will produce the majority of your desired outcome. This, combined with Chunking creates the Compounding Effect.

Engage the Compounding Effect in your Space of Productivity and you will truly become unstoppable.

#1 SPACE OF PRODUCTIVITY

Create your Space of Productivity by dedicating a space solely to practice, where nothing else besides practice or writing takes place. It should include whatever tools and resources you need so everytime you go to practice, you'll be able to easily enter a productive state.

As you use this space, you will establish a connection between it and Productivity, which will help you trigger this state quicker. As you reinforce this connection through perfected repetition, you'll Encode it [internalizing and automating the connection], while also developing a Habit. This means that the more you use this space, the faster you'll be able to enter a state of Productivity, and the deeper you'll be able to explore it.

Things to include:

- Guitar
- Amp
- Music Stand
- Recording Software [DAW]
- Metronome
- Anything else you need

Whatever you do, be consistent. Practice in the same place, and ideally at the same time each session. Have everything you need ready so you can sit down, warm up, and practice effectively. Don't waste time. Don't waste energy. Focus on creating results.

#2 COMPOUNDING EFFECT

As Practice Hackers, we want to focus on maximizing output while minimizing input. One of the best ways to do this is through the Compounding Effect which combines the 80/20 rule with Chunking.

The Old Framework is based on practicing tasks that are unrelated, switching between many of them in a session, and rarely sticking with any long enough to actually engage the Skill Development Zone. We cannot engage the Skill Development Zone unless we're at the height of Productivity. We cannot be at the height of Productivity if we're switching between too many tasks.

So for us to truly accelerate our progress, we need to minimize the number of tasks we're doing, focusing on the ones that are most likely to create our desired outcome [80/20]. We also need to combine similar tasks together in the same window of time, to minimize the cost of task-switching [Chunking].

What does this look like:

- Let's say your current practice session has 3 main aspects you're working on: Technique, Theory, and Creativity.
- With Technique, you're working on alternate picking, with Theory, you're working on the modes, and with Creativity you're working on songwriting.
- To engage the Compounding Effect, you could write a song, riff, or a solo using alternate picking and the modes.
- By working on everything like this, you're engaging multiple processes of learning, and maximizing your Productivity.

Note that the Compounding Effect is a more advanced strategy. However, the more you can see how everything connects and compliments each other, the more you can focus on the highest leverage tasks that will bring everything else up. It's a fun game to play.

HOW TO APPLY THIS

It doesn't have to be fancy or expensive, but establish your Space of Productivity. This could be a corner of your room, an area of the house, or somewhere else. Wherever it is, it needs to be a space you can be consistent with. Ensure you have all of the tools you need ready to use. Through repeated use of this space, you'll be able to enter states of Productivity quicker, and explore them in much greater depth. It will also be much easier to form a Habit.

To really maximize your Productivity, use the Compounding Effect, combining the 80/20 rule with Chunking.

> **Practice Hacker Tip:** Create your Space of Productivity and engage the Compounding Effect to accelerate your pathway to mastery.

BOOK II

THE FOOLPROOF SYSTEM FOR EASILY SETTING GOALS AND GAINING ACHIEVEMENT MOMENTUM

MINDSET. BELIEF. VISION

Secret 11

The Magnitude of Mindset and Belief

Mindset and Beliefs build the Foundation of the Temple.

When I was just starting out on guitar, I would stay up late watching different TV shows like MTV and Much Music, trying to discover new bands. I would go to the local music shop whenever I could to check out the guitars they had, and even listen to other guitarists. I would buy different CDs and DVDs that I would listen to and learn from religiously. For a while, I was even buying a new issue of Guitar World every month. Guitar was my life. There was no doubt at all that I would be a great guitarist one day. I would fantasize all day and all night. I saw myself on that stage, impacting the world. I felt it in my blood. The path was clear. Or so I thought.

When I hit that wall years ago, for the first time in my life I actually felt uncertainty about my path. I felt like every hope, ambition, and dream I had of being a great guitarist was on the brink of simply remaining a dream. I stopped progressing on guitar, I was stuck. I thought maybe

I just wasn't as talented as other people. Maybe I was getting too old. Maybe I just didn't have enough time to practice. Maybe I had reached my limit. Limiting Belief after Limiting Belief crowded my mind. It was frightening - I felt out of control.

I had never thought about giving up guitar before that, but I was stuck like this for years. I was pushing so hard to make my dreams come true, but nothing was changing. It was defeating. It was actually embarrassing. I was always talking to people about my dreams and the things I wanted to accomplish. Everyone was excited for me. Yet time was passing me by and I wasn't moving - still working the same minimum wage job, still in debt, and still broke. I honestly felt like a loser.

And that's when two paths revealed themselves to me.

Either I give up and just focus on living a regular life, getting a decent job and living in comfort and safety, or do anything it takes to make my dreams come true, and fulfill my destiny.

I reflected on the countless people I knew who gave up their dreams for a 'comfortable life' and in most I saw lifelessness. They regretted not pursuing their dreams. They regretted not taking chances. I didn't want to get to the end of my life wondering what could've been. I wanted to get to the end of my life and reflect on what was: the risks I took; the failures and the successes; the glory. All of it.

I knew that I couldn't let my dreams remain my dreams. I had to do whatever it took, no matter the cost, to make it happen. And I haven't looked back since.

That decision opened me up to an entirely new way of understanding life. It led me on a journey of self-discovery and self-realization that I didn't even know was possible. One of the first resources I came across early-on was Stefan James from Project Life Mastery, specifically his work on Mindset, Beliefs, and Vision. It changed everything for me. It provided me with a greater awareness of myself. I came to realize that the reason I didn't have the results I desired in life was because I wasn't the person I needed to be to create them. It was as simple as that.

This realization humbled me. For so long I thought that I couldn't change myself. I just thought that some people were born to have certain results in life. Some people just got 'lucky' and the rest of us have to suffer. But this just simply isn't the case. We can recreate ourselves, daily, and we need to - or else the world does it for us. We aren't as good as we can be. We can always become more. And there's something so exciting about that.

This realization was difficult at first - I really didn't want to hear it. But I knew that I didn't have a choice. If I ignored this information, my life would continue to spiral out of control. I would live a life of regret - always wondering what could've been. I would likely be full of anger and resentment, never being fulfilled in life. Others would likely suffer as well - people that I was meant to reach or impact in some way big or small. All because I didn't take control over my life; my dreams; my destiny.

I needed to become more. And it started with shifting my Mindset and Beliefs.

Mindset and Beliefs are like your brain's programming. They decide what information comes in, how it's filtered, and how it's organized. As a result, they dictate your thoughts and actions, effectively creating your life as you experience it.

Vision without **Mindset** = <u>Wasted Potential</u>
Mindset without **Vision** = <u>Limited Potential</u>

Dreams are goals without action. Don't let your dreams remain your dreams. You're fully capable of accomplishing what you desire, but you need to become more. You need to become the person who creates those results. This starts with your Mindset and your Beliefs.

STIMULUS - STORY - BELIEF - ACTION

STIMULUS

Simply put, life happens to you whether you like it or not. You can't always choose what happens to you, but you can always choose how you respond to it. The Stimulus that influences Belief can come from a lot of places: environment, experiences, people, events, current knowledge, the past, the future, and more.

STORY

Memories aren't truly objective representations of experiences you've had, but rather how you felt about them - unless you have a photographic memory. However, this emotional experience shapes your interpretation of what happens and therefore, the Story you tell yourself about it.

BELIEF

This Story forms a Belief, whether accurate or not. Often, this is to protect the ego from harm. Our brains desire to pull us towards pleasure and protect us from pain. So these Beliefs technically serve a purpose - but not usually in a way that's empowering or in our control.

ACTION

Belief is the Foundation on which all Action is carried out, even if you're unconscious of it.

Do you see how dangerous it is to not be in control of the **Stimulus - Story - Belief - Action** sequence? This is the issue most people face: they are unaware of this process, therefore, they become its victim. Most people are reactive, not proactive. So if your response to life's chaos is reactionary, guess what? Your life will breed more chaos.

However, a proactive approach allows you to benefit from any situation or event. It allows you to live above the natural laws that sway you between positive and negative experiences. They give you control over your life, through the power of transmutation. Personally, this has been one of the greatest gifts I've received in life: the ability to take any event or circumstance and find a way to benefit from it.

The results you currently have in life are due to your framework, and a key part of your framework is the set of Beliefs you have and operate from. But you're not alone in this. Most people have Beliefs and frameworks that don't serve them - some to greater degrees than others. The beautiful thing though, is now that you have awareness, you can change your results by changing your framework. But first, you need to change your Beliefs.

THE IMPORTANCE OF MINDSET AND BELIEFS

SUCCESSFUL vs UNSUCCESSFUL

Have you noticed there are some people whose entire life is full of suffering, yet they somehow find great happiness, joy, purpose, and most importantly - fulfilment? So much so, that they are often able to ascend from their personal hell, into better lives for them and their families? Even inspiring others along the way?

Have you also noticed there are some people who are born into what we'd consider 'privilege,' yet are unfulfilled, depressed, and without purpose or passion? These people often end their own lives or resort to destructive behaviours like drug abuse or alcoholism.

What is the key difference between these types of people?

You could say environment, role models, spiritual outlook, family, childhood, trauma, and a plethora of other unique circumstances - but you'd be only partially correct. I believe there's one key factor above all else:

Belief
[the stories you tell yourself]

YOUR PROGRAMMING

Your Beliefs inform your Mindset. They create or destroy Vision for your life. They define your meaning and purpose. They cultivate values. They filter and shape the experiences you have. They open or close possibilities.

Religions, institutions, corporations, and governments are all based around some set of Beliefs - usually in the form of Values. We come together as a nation based on a shared set of Beliefs. We often form friendships and relationships based on shared Beliefs.

What we need to do is come to understand something:

Our Beliefs _can_ be changed - they need to <u>serve</u> us

Our Beliefs act as the programming our brains use to filter, organize, and understand information. By shifting our Beliefs, we change how we interpret information, therefore we change how we think and act.

Our Beliefs exist whether we participate in their creation or not. So if we're in a position in life we don't want to be in, the first thing we have to do is change our Beliefs about what's possible. We need to change our Beliefs about ourselves. We can control Beliefs. They don't need to control us. They should support us towards our Vision; the outcome we want for our life.

LIMITING BELIEFS

PLAYING NOT TO LOSE

A lot of people's Beliefs are rooted in avoiding loss or failure. They are afraid of failure, so they don't even try - or they just pass by, hoping to avoid pain. In doing so, they also avoid the potential for success. Or they've lowered their standard for success so low that anything that isn't complete failure is 'success.' By doing this, they close off opportunities. They assume they will fail, and so they do.

This is called playing not to lose. It's being 'safe,' it's being 'cautious,' and ultimately, it's protecting the ego. But unfortunately, this is where growth stops, and suffering continues.

As William Shakespeare once said, 'Our doubts are traitors.' And he was right.

EGO

When we experience an event, we tell ourselves stories based on how we feel about it. We justify why things happen, we put up boundaries. It's all to protect ourselves.

See how this can be problematic though? What if you were trying to learn something new, like a new song or riff, and it was too difficult so you gave up? Or maybe you wanted to perform live but you flopped a few times and as a result you stopped performing? Or maybe you put out a song you were really proud of but people didn't like it, so you stopped recording and releasing music?

Even outside of guitar, what if you approached someone you were attracted to and got shut down so you stopped approaching people? What if you tried to lose weight but failed the first time so you never tried again?

For many, the path stops here. Failure is difficult to deal with, especially when approaching something new, which takes a lot of courage to begin with. Instead of staying focused on your Goal and outcome, if you experience failure and give up, you'll never be able to achieve what you desire. To me, giving up is the greatest failure of all. At least if you're failing *towards* something, you're learning.

Ego plays an important role in our human experience, but it can also hold us back.

In terms of music practice, there are two main types of motivation:

- Personal Improvement (task, process, learning, mastery)
- Social Comparison (ego, ability, outcome, performance)

  - Ego-approach: demonstrating a high ability to others

  - Ego-avoid: avoiding demonstrating a lack of ability to others

Personal Improvement goals are highly effective in motivating practice whereas Social Comparison tends to be negative, especially after failure. It may contribute to lower interest, disorganization, and shallow involvement in learning strategies. Though you can certainly use Social Comparison in terms of competition or challenges, it's not really sustainable or healthy on its own. It's like a rollercoaster; extreme highs and extreme lows.

The biggest obstacle you'll face along your pathway to mastery is in comparing yourself to others. Everyone has their own path, they operate from their own frameworks. Some are more effective than yours, sure, but you should use the success of others as Inspiration and not as a measurement against your own success. You can't change or improve what you can't measure - and you can't measure yourself against others. However, you *can* measure against yourself. There's always someone better. Grow at the quickest rate you can, keep on learning, and become better today than you were yesterday.

Something to keep in mind: you're likely somebody that other people compare themselves to, wishing they were as good as you. This goes both ways. So get out of that limiting Mindset and focus on the task at hand: becoming the guitarist you've always dreamed of being and impacting the world with your music. Compare only to yourself. Be inspired by others.

THE QUESTIONS YOU ASK YOURSELF

You can't always control situations, but you can control how you respond to them. As the saying goes: whether you can or you can't - you're right. Your Beliefs determine your actions and your outcome. Many people use limiting statements like 'I can't' or 'I don't know how.' By using these types of statements, they close off potential answers or the ability to grow. They create Limiting Beliefs.

Remember how the brain is a computer, and you can program it? If you're programming it with definitive statements of fact [closed loops], then your brain has no reason to look for other answers. It hasn't been programmed to do so.

When in a hurtful situation, people don't often ask themselves how they can benefit from it; what they can learn, how they can grow; if there was anything they could've done differently. I get it, it's difficult. But you know what's more difficult? Suffering - especially more than necessary. What benefit is there to allow situations or even people to control you and wreak havoc in your life? Why give them that much power over you?

We naturally try to avoid suffering. Some people even go as far as removing any 'positive' emotion in their life so they don't have to feel suffering in its absence. They believe it's better to be numb or to suffer all the time. But what kind of life is that? Suffering is a part of existence, yes, but you can either let it control you or you can control how you respond to it. What do you choose?

I'd rather have control over my life and how I respond to the events that shape it. I'd rather find a way to benefit from every situation than to have it control the way I think, feel, and act. I'm sure you feel the same way. The questions we ask ourselves and our self-talk is a huge way we form the Stories and the Beliefs in our minds. Are you using degrading language? Saying that you suck, that you're terrible, that you'll never amount to anything? Or do you encourage yourself and build yourself up? Recognizing failures but seeing them as opportunities to grow? Asking yourself how you can benefit from even the most dire of situations?

Negative self-talk will tear you apart from the inside out. It will destroy your life on many levels. However, positive self-talk opens up opportunities. It encourages you to learn and grow. You're able to recognize mistakes, see them as a learning experience, and move on. It's not living in ignorance or fantasy - you're changing your perception of events, which changes your Beliefs and therefore your life.

If you want positive results in life, you need to transform negative situations and thoughts into those you can benefit from. You need to create and live by Empowering Beliefs.

EMPOWERING BELIEFS

PLAYING TO WIN

Instead of Beliefs founded in avoiding loss or failure, what if your Beliefs were rooted in the process of becoming more; learning through failure and taking risks? It would become a lifestyle. Every failure would simply show you something new you had to learn. As a result, you would experience success. A lot of it. Not as the focus, but as a reward for becoming more.

Think of the world of fitness. Most people who desire to eat healthy or exercise for a 'Goal' rarely achieve it, and if they do, they often fall back into old Habits shortly after. Why? Because they are focused on the result and not the process. They create a negative association with the changes needed to attain their Goal and therefore the process feels like punishment. Then, when they reach it, they often go back into comfort, which is what got them into trouble in the first place. Sound familiar?

Compare this to someone who makes fitness a lifestyle. By creating a Habit around healthy eating and exercise, growth never stops. They're immersed in the process of becoming more. Every failure or obstacle is a lesson. Everything is a chance for growth. As a result, they are able to easily achieve their desired outcome. Most importantly, they are able to continue growing - establishing higher Foundations and achieving even greater outcomes. This is playing to win.

See how this opens up opportunities? You're more likely to take risks. You recognize failure as a part of the journey. You know you will win at some point, you simply need to learn more. You need to become more. This is a key difference between the world's most successful people and the average.

WHAT DOES SUCCESS MEAN TO YOU?

If we know the key difference between successful people and the average is their Beliefs, then what Beliefs do successful people have that the average don't?

As Tony Robbins outlines in his book, *Unlimited Power*, there are Seven 'Lies' of Success that many of the world's most successful people tell themselves. He calls them lies because they might not reflect reality in a purely objective, realistic, or logical sense. Life can feel chaotic and events can be hard to explain - but if you can find a way to benefit from anything that happens to you - you become a master of reality.

Here are the Seven Lies of Success:

1. Everything happens for a reason and a purpose, and it serves us
2. There is no such thing as failure, only results
3. Whatever happens, take responsibility
4. It's not necessary to understand everything to be able to use everything
5. People are your greatest resource
6. Work is play

7. There's no abiding success without commitment

At the end of the day, it's simple: those with success took control over their lives. They did whatever it took. They immersed themselves in the process. They made the sacrifices needed. They found a way to benefit from every situation. They made it happen.

Despite their upbringing, despite any tragedy, despite any handicaps or hardships - they had the Belief that they would be successful no matter what. There obviously needs to be more than *just* Belief, but Belief is the gateway for opportunity. It's the Foundation for everything in your life. The stronger the Foundation, the higher you can build off of it.

If we seek success in any area of life, we need to know if our current Belief system is holding us back or if it's supporting us.

When I ask you to think about the word success - what does it mean to you? Money, fame? Perhaps more 'noble' notions like family, loyalty, and happiness?

There are no wrong answers, just be honest with yourself.

Whatever success means to you, you need to be able to pursue it. The success you seek is often rooted in much deeper desires, such as your purpose. The more you see and understand these connections, the greater your Motivation will be to achieve success. Never put yourself in a position where you don't have the control to create the success you desire. If you do find yourself in that position, it's likely because of your Beliefs or other parts of your framework. Change your Beliefs. Change your framework. Change your results.

The only person holding you back from pursuing and achieving success is **you**. No person, no government, no institution, no mythical creature, no religion - you. You, and only you.

So what are you going to do about it?

FAIL MORE, FAIL BETTER

How many times have you failed at something? I'm assuming a lot. We all have.

Guess what. Successful people have failed more. I use the term 'fail' lightly. Successful people don't see failure as definite. They don't see it as the end of the road or an obstacle they can't overcome. It's a stepping stone. They don't let failure stop them.

Through many attempts, they learned to fail better. They figured out what worked and what didn't, which is a critical aspect of self-regulation and therefore - mastery. When others quit, they didn't, and as a result they achieved success. In the process, they became a more capable, developed, and experienced individual. They became more.

In the process of discovery, they found better frameworks to operate from. Frameworks that created their desired results and that were repeated and refined.

I cannot overstate this: their success did not happen overnight. Very rarely is this ever the case, and if it is - it's usually very short-lived. Why? Because without a strong Foundation to build the pillars of your life upon, the weight of success will cause all of it to crumble. It can't be supported. It doesn't have the levels or the structures needed. A good example of this is with lottery winners.

Lottery winners aren't bad people, but without developing the traits required to earn the type of money they receive, they rarely know how to handle it in a sustainable way. It's like giving kids dynamite. Because of that, most of them are back to square one within a year or so - or in a worse situation.

Success is earned, not given. And by becoming who we need to be in order to cultivate success, we gain a new perspective on life and a deeper appreciation for it. We are able to handle it. We have the skills and knowledge we need; we have a strong Foundation to build the pillars of our life upon. A Foundation that can easily hold the weight of success.

It's not an easy process, but it's a process worth pursuing. Not only for yourself, but for others. The greater the success you have in life, whatever that means to you, the more you can serve others as well.

So keep in mind that failure is a part of the process. Truly successful people created their success by not accepting failure as the 'end' of their journey, but as something new they had to learn to achieve their dream. Their Beliefs carried them to success, through hell into paradise. They knew they could do it. Even if they didn't have the skills at the time, or the money, or anything else. They found the books, the resources, the people, the opportunities - whatever it was. They made it happen.

Sometimes, this might take a few months, sometimes it might even take a few years or nearly an entire lifetime. A good example of this is the story of Colonel Sanders, the founder of KFC. I won't go into the whole story here but he had a very tragic life, eventually retiring around 65 and was dirt poor. All he had to his name was a chicken recipe that he created and perfected. He lived in his car for 2 years, travelling around trying to sell his recipe to anyone who would buy it.

Want to know how many times he was rejected? 1009. Let that sink in. Most people would've given up after the first few tries - if they even got that far. But once he found somebody willing to work out a deal, the rest is history and KFC has become one of the largest fast-food franchises in the world.

The fact that success isn't instant can be daunting for a lot of people, especially if we're only outcome-focused. If we see work as play then as we're working towards our Goals, the *process* becomes enjoyable. The achievement of Goals are just stepping stones indicating growth, but the Goals aren't the only focus. It's who we become in the process, it's the lifestyle, it's the transformation.

By not taking risks, by not failing, by not learning, by playing not to lose, and by not playing to win - you might avoid *some* risk in life. But realistically, you're taking the biggest risk of all. You're risking never accomplishing what you truly desire in life. You're risking your dreams. You're risking your destiny.

Do you want to get to the end of your life and look back at it, wondering what could've been if only you kept on your dreams? Never live in regrets.

No matter your intelligence, your upbringing, your language, your culture, or your abilities right now - you can always be more than you are, and there's something so exciting about that. You can always grow. You can always learn something new.

This is actually a defining trait of successful people - they are constantly in a state of learning; reading, thinking, taking courses, and finding mentors. The second you think you know it all - you lose. Those who have the success you desire aren't better than you, they just know more than you do right now - at least enough to create the results they have; the results you want.

Accept failure as part of the road to success. Learn to fail more. Learn to fail better. Make it a lifestyle and you won't have to worry about success in any area of your life again.

THE FIVE WHYS

One of the greatest lessons I've learned on my journey is that by asking yourself better questions, you tend to find better answers. You know a lot more than you think you do, and if you don't have the answers right now, you'll have a better idea of where to find them. Most people close off the chance of finding answers by using limiting language, usually in the form of Limiting Beliefs, as we've previously discussed. This is why it's so important to ask yourself better questions.

In most cases, asking better questions will be enough to get the answers you need. But sometimes you might need to go deeper, and a great method for that is the Five Whys technique.

- If you find yourself in a situation you need answers to [troubleshooting, problem-solving, etc.], ask yourself 'why?'
- Give as specific of an answer as you can, and repeat the question.
- Keep on doing this until you've asked 5 times total, or you have discovered the root cause of the issue

Normally, asking yourself why something happened can be dangerous. It's a vague question and often leads to negative answers. If you're struggling, your brain might say it's because you can't do it, or because you're not smart enough. These answers are defeating and aren't productive. We want to empower ourselves towards success, so continue to dive deeper until you truly discover the answers.

The more specific the question you ask yourself, the more accurate the answer you'll receive. To identify the root cause of a problem, consider the Five Whys technique.

TRANSMUTATION OF BELIEFS [FROM NEGATIVE TO POSITIVE]

So, you are starting to understand the importance of Mindset and Beliefs. They are the Foundation for your Vision. They are the Foundation for your life. But you might be asking: how do I change Limiting Beliefs and how do I create or use Empowering Beliefs?

Good question!

There are many ways to create Empowering Beliefs, but the first thing you have to do is recognize your Limiting Beliefs. Here are some examples of Limiting Beliefs you might have:

- I don't have enough time to practice
- I don't know how to practice

- I don't know where to begin
- I don't know what to practice
- I'll never be a great guitarist
- I don't have money to invest in my success as a guitarist
- I'm not as good or talented as _____
- I'm too old/young
- I already know everything
- I can't focus on practicing guitar
- I don't have [insert gear here] so I can't get better

See how defeating these are? They close off everything. They are definitive. They are final. They are statements of 'fact' to your brain.

In the process of changing Limiting Beliefs, the first step is self-awareness. As you go about your life, catch yourself as you're responding to situations or thoughts. Do your responses sound like the previous examples? If so, they are likely Limiting Beliefs.

Watch how you'll begin to develop a better sense of your reactions which will lead you to be more proactive - gaining control over your thoughts and actions. The quicker you develop this self-awareness, the quicker you can change your Beliefs, and therefore your life.

Taking the previous examples, here are some ways we can shift the Beliefs from **Limiting** to **Empowering** through a process I call **Transmutation** - which is a fancy way of saying through changing or shifting.

- **Original:** I don't have enough time to practice

  - **New:** How can I make time for practice? How can I maximize the output of each session [results] while minimizing the input [time]?

- **Original:** I don't know how to practice

  - **New:** What's the most effective way to practice? How do the best musicians practice?

- **Original:** I don't know where to begin

  - **New:** What master or mentor can I learn from? How can I Make their Pinnacle my Foundation?

- **Original:** I don't know what to practice

  - **New:** Based on my Vision, what Goals or skills are most likely to help me get there?

- **Original:** I'll never be a great guitarist

  - **New:** What is responsible for creating a great guitarist? How can I hack that process and focus on what produces results, without wasting time or energy?

- **Original:** I don't have money to invest in my success as a guitarist

  - **New:** I'm wasting thousands of dollars a year on lessons, resources, books, courses, and even new guitars - trying to play better. What can I invest in that will help me get more out of my practice, in less time, so I save money?

- **Original:** I'm not as good or talented as _____

  - **New:** ____ is incredible, they are so inspiring! How can I learn from them, or improve myself with their frameworks?

- **Original:** I'm too old/young

  - **New:** I'm motivated to get the most progress and value I can out of the guitar - how do I do that without wasting time, energy, and money?

- **Original:** I already know everything

  - **New:** I'm hungry to learn! I want to learn everything I can - what do others know that I don't?

- **Original:** I can't focus on practicing guitar
  - **New:** What's getting in the way of my focus? How can I work on improving that? How can I adjust my practice to focus better?

- **Original:** I don't have [insert gear here] so I can't get better
  - **New:** Good gear is important, but how can I get the most out of the gear that I have?

Even though some of these Transmutations appear a little cheesy, I'm sure you get the point. Additionally, you can use Empowering Language to enhance your Beliefs, such as:

- I can _____
- I am great at _____
- I have _____ NOW
- I am capable of _____

Confidence comes from competence, but competence starts with believing you *can* do something, followed by doing it. Form Beliefs that support the outcome you desire by positioning it like you already have it [like an Affirmation]. Your intentions for the future will shape your present moment. It will become a self-fulfilling prophecy.

Don't make excuses for yourself that hold you back from pursuing success with guitar, or in any area of your life. Don't allow the fear of failure to hold you back from your potential. Guitar is such an incredible skill and experience. In fact, music is the Foundation for human civilization; it's a universal language, and you get to push that forward in your own unique way. Music transcends culture and time. It's a part of the fabric of nations; and the very fabric of our reality. It's intrinsic to who we are, who we have always been, and who we will be in the future. And you, no matter the skill level, hold that force within you.

Maybe you don't want to be a rockstar or a full-time professional musician. But if nothing else, you should be able to become the guitarist you've always dreamed of being without having to practice all day. By starting with guitar, you'd be surprised at how much these processes can affect other areas of your life. Once you become immersed in the process, creating a lifestyle around becoming more, it's hard to go back. Joy, freedom, growth, and potential await you. You simply need to begin walking the path.

You're responsible for the life you have, based on the stories you tell yourself. Time to create new stories!

HOW TO APPLY THIS

So we've identified how critical your Mindset and Beliefs are to your success on guitar and in life, so what's next?

1. Make a list of 5-10 Limiting Beliefs. They can be the ones previously mentioned or others. Be as specific as you can. They need to be real, and need to mean something to you.

2. Transmute those Limiting Beliefs into Empowering Beliefs. Use open-ended questions like 'how can I?' and use the Five Whys technique to go deeper. Be as specific as you can.

3. Take on the Seven Lies of Success

   - Everything happens for a reason and a purpose, and it serves us

   - There is no such thing as failure. There are only results

   - Whatever happens, take responsibility

   - It's not necessary to understand everything to be able to use everything

   - People are your greatest resource

   - Work is play

- There's no abiding success without commitment

4. Include any additional Empowering Beliefs you feel will aid you in your journey.

- Include Empowering Language such:

    - I can _____
    - I am great at _____
    - I have _____ NOW
    - I am capable of _____

Empowering Beliefs can be a beacon of hope when all hope seems lost. Even if your Beliefs have elements of being unrealistic, if they pull you from the darkest depths of suffering and propel you into greatness and fulfillment, then they are Beliefs worth keeping.

Success lies at the end of suffering. Many people get stuck and give up before they get to experience glory. But not you - not anymore.

If you can turn a negative situation into a positive one, you win. In my opinion, this is one of the greatest secrets to life.

> **Practice Hacker Tip:** Master the mind, master reality. Cultivate Beliefs that keep you growing and engaged with the process of becoming more, and success will come naturally.

Secret 12

Vision [Macro and Micro]

Our future intentions shape our present moment. Vision guides our path, it is our destination. For guitar, there are 2 types of vision: Macro and Micro.

Throughout most of my life, I never valued education. I always associated learning with school - just something I 'had' to do until I got older. I think a lot of people fall into this category. I didn't understand the importance of continued learning and personal growth. I didn't know I could better myself. I didn't know I could change myself. It wasn't until I was on the brink of giving up guitar and music, that I was willing to do whatever it took. I had to become more, I had to become the person capable of creating the results I desired.

To achieve this, I knew that I couldn't just rely on myself; I couldn't do it on my own. In fact, trying to do it that way is what got me into the position I was in. My results were because of my framework. So I needed to look outside of myself. I needed a New Framework.

This began my obsession with reading and self-education; trying to understand the world around me as well as within me. Ultimately, trying to understand what produces results. To become more, we have to know more. To know more, we have to learn more.

Over the years I've read a lot of interesting books, but there's one book in particular that had a profound impact on me. Some things I agree with and some I don't, but that's the beautiful thing about learning: you're constantly challenging and reassessing your own Beliefs. You're sharpening your critical thinking skills. You're coming to understand the world around you better. You're also coming to understand yourself better. As a result, life begins to open up in entirely new ways.

The book was by a hypnotherapist named Dolores Canon. She was well known for her past-life and regressive hypnotherapy work, and whether you believe such things are real or not, her books are definitely interesting. In the particular book I read, there was a discussion around the idea that our intentions for our future, create our future. In other words, imagining your future manifests it.

This has been an idea that I've heard floating around for a long time, and always had difficulty understanding and accepting. It felt partially correct, but I knew something was missing. *How* was this going to happen exactly? Was I just supposed to wait around and hope for things to change? It just didn't connect. It didn't make sense to me.

I believe this is what a lot of people do when they have a 'dream' of the life they want for themselves. They imagine it, even with conviction, but that's all they do. It exists purely in their mind, with no grounding in reality. Then, the years begin to pass, and life around them begins to change - but they don't. They remain the same. They do what they have always done, getting what they have always gotten. Any hope of achieving their dreams begins to fade away. Hour by hour. Day by day.

However, in the book there was a solution offered which flipped this perspective on its head and changed everything for me. It's not that our intentions for the future create our future, it's that **our intentions for the future shape our present moment.**

I'll say that again: **our intentions for the future shape our present moment.**

When I read this, it stopped me dead in my tracks. I was completely blown away. It's such a simple concept and seems almost outrageous because of how obvious it is. But for years, my problem was that I wasn't engaging with my own path. I had stopped learning. I had stopped growing. I was just doing what was needed to get by. I was reactionary - all of life's chaos becoming my own. Because I wasn't changing, nothing around me was changing. All of my hopes and dreams simply existed in my mind. But this completed the understanding. This was the key.

To achieve your Vision, you need to become more. But to become more, you need to calibrate your daily actions in alignment with your Vision.

I cannot overstate just how profound this idea was for me, and still is. This finally unlocked movement in my life. It allowed me to begin making my Vision; my dream a reality. One step at a time, I was able to progress towards becoming the person I needed to be to create the results I desired. All because each day I was becoming more - I was calibrating action in accordance with my Vision.

Mindset and Beliefs are the Foundation of what's possible. Vision guides the pathway towards it.

MACRO VISION

The best way to create a Vision is to start with any big Goal, hope, or aspiration you have. It may be vague to begin with, or detailed, but start with what's currently on your mind, then expand off of it. The hardest part is starting. Once you get a few initial ideas out, it becomes much easier to add to the list. Don't overthink it, you just want to get the wheels turning. If needed, set a timer for 10 minutes and write out as many ideas as you can. You can always go back later to add, remove, or refine them.

Ultimately, your Vision is your dream-world: what life would be like if you had everything you ever wanted. Right now, we'll mostly focus on your Vision as it relates to guitar, but I highly encourage that you repeat this same process for your life as a whole. You'll only benefit from it. This is how you become proactive. This is how you take control of your life and your destiny. The clearer your Vision, the more accurate you can calibrate daily action towards creating it.

So, what is your dream-world as a guitarist? What does becoming the guitarist of your dreams look like?

Here are some questions you might want to ask yourself:

- What does being a guitarist mean to me?
- What kind of lifestyle would I have?
- What kind of impact would I have on others?
- What kind of music would I be able to learn or even create?
- What type of band would I be in?
- Would I be touring around the world? What bands would I be touring with?
- Would I be on the cover of magazines?
- Would I have my own website or YouTube channel? How many followers would I have?
- What kind of fulfilment would I get out of life by having mastery over guitar? How would that make me feel?
- Would I just play guitar as a hobby, sharing that with my friends and family?
- Would I be a guitar teacher? Locally, or at a University or Music Academy?

- What guitar skills would I have? How good would I be at them? What would that provide me?

- Are there people who have the results that I want? Who are they, and what are those results? What experience would that give me to have those results?

There are obviously many more questions you can ask yourself, as this process of discovery is personal and subjective. However, the goal here is to pull out as much detail as you can regarding your Vision, so it feels real and excites you. Immerse yourself in it. This is your future.

Now, the next step is key. Understand that this dream reality you have for yourself is linked to deeply-rooted desires. It's my Belief that these desires are connected to a deeper meaning or purpose in your life. Whatever your desires are, discover the deeper meaning or purpose behind them and use them to your advantage to create a better world for yourself and for others.

For example, if a part of your dream reality is desiring to be 'famous,' on the surface this might seem like a purely ego-driven idea. However, if you dive deeper, you might discover that you see it as a way to impact people on a higher level; inspiring them and improving their lives in some way with your art and influence.

So - what do you believe your purpose is, in music or otherwise? How does your purpose impact yourself or others? What does life look like if this purpose is fulfilled? You may not have the answers right now, but this is the core of who you are as a person, and as a guitarist. Every part of your life stems from this, so you need to get clear on it and truly understand it. What you perceive as your purpose will become the Foundation of your Vision. It will dictate who you're capable of becoming.

I firmly believe everyone has a unique purpose in life. You have a unique hole to fill in the world. However, if you don't, it's not that life goes on as normal - you actually leave a hole just as big as the one you were meant to fill.

So with that in mind, what is the absolute worst-case scenario if you don't pursue your goals on guitar or in music?

Some questions to ask yourself:

- What would life look like if I failed to reach my potential?
- What would life look like if I failed to fulfill my purpose?
- How much would it hurt those I am meant to impact or inspire? Whose lives I'm meant to change?
- What regrets would I have at the end of my life? Would I reflect back on what was, or what could've been?
- How would it feel watching others pass me by, living my dream while I sit on the sidelines?
- How unfulfilled would I feel?
- How would it feel to never create the music I always wanted to create? Or learn the songs I always wanted to learn?
- How would I feel if I was never able to tour or even play a show?
- How would I feel if I was never able to be in a band?

Now, you're probably wondering why this seems so extreme. It's just guitar! What do you mean I have a purpose with guitar and that the world will suffer if I don't fulfill it?

As I've stated previously, music is one of the most incredible parts of being human. Whether you want to be a professional musician or just want to improve for yourself, there is serious power and fulfilment in guitar. Music is a universal language, and you speak it. Many people wish they could be like you. They already look up to you - you just don't know it yet.

Like with anything in life, we're constantly pulled between darkness and light. Generally, we move towards that which makes us feel whole, complete, happy, and fulfilled, while we push away from that which removes us from these feelings.

If we establish a clear Vision of the 'light' of pursuing our Goals, then we have a defined target we're inspired to hit. The issue is that anything worth pursuing or having often requires suffering, sacrifice, and growth to attain.

Think of this process like a mini version of the Hero's Journey. You're going from the known, into the unknown; fighting, battling, and overcoming adversity. Sometimes, the end-goal isn't enough of a motivator to go through all of that suffering and potential failure, so many people tend to avoid it. Understandably so. It's easier to sit around and watch TV or eat ice cream than it is to do something meaningful.

This is why it's critical to understand the opposite of your Vision; what happens if you don't pursue it. It's not that inaction will leave you neutral and the world will go on without you. It's that you will leave a hole in the world just as big as you were meant to fill. Right now, you're in-between darkness and light. Either your dreams will remain your dreams, and everyone suffers for it [yourself and those you were meant to impact], or you'll achieve your potential; becoming more - making the world a better and brighter place as a result.

Awareness has removed the divide. It's up to you to choose your side and to begin walking the path.

Imagine you wanted to be in a band but you didn't think you were good enough. You truly felt this was your purpose in life, but you were struggling to make it work. You tried to practice but you weren't making progress and it was defeating. Instead of finding a way to make it work and following through on the Vision you had for yourself, you gave up because it was too difficult. You'd prefer just to play video games or watch movies or hang out with friends.

But what if there was one kid who could've heard the music you wrote? What if he had been inspired to pick up the guitar because of you and it changed his life forever? Giving him an outlet for expression, instead of turning to destructive behaviours? Or what if you were in a band that wrote a certain song that saved somebody's life? Now imagine if you gave up instead. Asides from the unfulfillment and regret you would feel for not pursuing your purpose, which would affect every other area of your life, would that one kid ever end up playing guitar? Would his life be changed? And the other kid, would he still be alive?

I understand these are hypothetical situations and a little intense, but I'm trying to outline that even small, minute actions can have a massive effect on a global scale. Often far beyond what we think is possible. This is also known as the butterfly effect.

So, if you feel driven towards something in life, in music or otherwise, to me this is an indication of your path and purpose. Dive deeper. Discover everything you can. Develop this into your Vision. You might not have the full picture right now, but as you begin walking your path, it will reveal itself to you. Each step you take will open up new doors; new opportunities, and everything will begin to unfold. You don't need to know everything right now, but get as clear on your Vision [your destination] as you can, so you can begin walking your path. You can make corrections, adjustments, and modifications as you go, but you'll never achieve your Vision unless you take those first steps. You need to stay in motion. You need to take action.

You must pursue your Vision at all costs. You must pursue your life purpose. You must pursue what excites you deep down; what breathes life into you and gives life meaning. Even if all of the circumstances around your Vision aren't 100% logical, it's important to keep this perspective and use it to propel you into greatness. Not only for yourself, but for those you're meant to impact.

This Vision for yourself becomes your Macro Vision. It's your overall Vision for yourself as a guitarist. It basically outlines your dream world; who you want to be, what you want to experience, the impact you want to have, and much more. It also identifies the opposite.

The next step is to divide your Macro Vision across the 3 Fundamental Aspects of Guitar. This is what we'll refer to as your Micro Vision.

MICRO VISION

Our Macro Vision is the summary of who we want to be as a guitarist. Our Micro Vision is more detailed and specific. We will create one for each of the 3 Fundamental Aspects of Guitar.

TECHNIQUE

What do you desire to learn and accomplish with Technique? Think of the types of Techniques, the speed, the clarity. Are there examples of other guitarists who you aspire to be like? Are there specific songs you want to learn how to play? What else can you include? Get as specific as possible.

THEORY

What skills within Theory do you want to master? Modes? Chords? Harmony? Are there certain guitarists or songs that represent the level you want to be at? What else can you include? Be as detailed as you can.

CREATIVITY

Are you looking to improvise like a certain guitarist you look up to? Or maybe write songs on a similar level as a band you love? Include everything you can here as well, the more detailed the better.

With each of these Fundamental Aspects of Guitar, list what you truly desire with as much detail as you can. The more specific you are, the more likely you'll be to achieve what you desire. Don't just include random information because it sounds good or other people say you should learn it. This information needs to reflect what *you* want to accomplish as a guitarist - at least to the best of your current knowledge. You need to be genuinely driven towards it. Your Vision [Macro and Micro] is going to guide all decisions you make. It will shape the guitarist you become. Do **not** take this lightly.

Once you have your Micro Vision established, rate each area out of 10, based on where you're **currently** at. This is critical. We need to continually measure ourselves against our standard. This is a part of how we're going to track progress.

Be brutally honest with yourself. This will help you focus on the particular areas you need to improve on and will help you adjust your strategy accordingly. You don't want to treat everything evenly if one area is suffering over the others. Think of lifting weights. If one body part is struggling to grow at the rate of the others, are you going to train all of them the same? No. You'll put extra focus on the lagging body part, while still working on the rest. Our aim here is to even out all areas and build them up to a 10/10 ranking.

Your Pillar of Specialization deals with your unique pathway on guitar; your contribution, your voice. This is linked to your Macro Vision. Your Micro Vision deals with the 3 areas of that pathway. All of this works together to create the guitarist you've always dreamed of being. It makes the destination clear so you can begin walking the path.

CHECKING IN

As I mentioned before - when you begin to walk to the path, that's when doors start to open. With this in mind, your Macro and Micro Vision will likely change and evolve over time. Your Vision is who you want to become, based on who you currently are. As you take action towards your Vision, who you currently are will change. As a result, so will your Vision.

This is why it's critical to check in on your progress and your Vision.

We'll go over this more in **Secret 18**, but the typical length I recommend for a practice program is 8 weeks. After those 8 weeks, revisit your Vision [Macro and Micro] and make adjustments as needed. Has your rating for each area changed? Is there anything you can add or remove to your Vision [Macro or Micro]? Is there anything you can further refine?

Consider taking notes and reflecting on what went well and what didn't. What can you improve on for next time?

This reflection is a critical Habit to develop and should only take you a few minutes. It helps remind you of what you're doing and why you're doing it. It also helps you understand if you're actually making progress. Many people aren't aware of the process so they aren't aware of their progress. Review your Vision often [ideally every 8 weeks] to help remind you of your destination, as well as the progress you're making towards it. Focus on what's working. Remove what isn't. Stay focused.

VISION + ACTION = SUCCESS

Success, true success, doesn't come to those who aren't ready. The most successful people in the world first had a Belief of what was possible and then created and held a Vision of what they desired. This Vision calibrated their path as they travelled it, and established the framework they now operate from to create the results they have.

Consider an athlete who has always believed they would compete at the Olympics. They held strongly to that Vision their entire life, and in each waking moment they worked towards it. Maybe they weren't as genetically gifted as others. Maybe they even suffered tragedy and misfortune, but they never gave up. They wanted it more than anything. They struggled, they failed, but they held true to their Vision. They took daily action towards it and calibrated their path. They did whatever it took. As a result, they got to stand on that podium; gold medal in hand, their dream fulfilled. They can look back on their life and reflect on what was, not what could've been.

Compare that to someone who was born with great genetics or 'privilege.' Maybe they were told their whole life how great they were and how successful they would be. As a result, they always assumed they would get to the Olympics, but never seriously worked towards it. They never held that Vision strong. They never had conviction. Without taking daily action and calibrating their path, they never reached their potential. They never got to compete. They never stood on that podium. Instead, they are stuck living a life of regret - reflecting on what could've been instead of what was.

I'm sure you're aware of countless success stories [or failures] that align with the above examples. In fact, there are likely people you know in your own life that fall into either category. There are always going to be people who have advantages over you, just like you have over others. But whatever your situation in life, know that you have the power and the ability to change it. Get clear on your Vision and revisit it often. This will guide your daily actions along the pathway to your success.

HOW TO APPLY THIS

Establish your Macro Vision as a guitarist. This is the overall vision for what you want; the best-case scenario. Additionally, include what will happen if you don't follow through with it; the worst-case scenario.

Establish your Micro Vision for each of the 3 Fundamental Aspects of Guitar: Technique, Theory, and Creativity. Get specific. Include skills, songs, guitarists, bands, and anything else you can think of.

Rate each area of your Micro Vision out of 10.

If you're struggling to explore ideas, set a timer for 10 minutes and write out as many ideas as you can for your Vision. They don't have to be well thought-out or hyper-detailed right now, just get the ideas flowing. Even if you only get 1 idea out - just *start*. Spill your thoughts onto the page. Revisit, explore, and refine them later.

Revisit your Vision [Macro and Micro] at the end of each 8-week program. Adjust your rating, refine your Vision, note what you can improve on, and continue pushing forward.

Practice Hacker Tip: Your intentions for the future shape your present moment. Get clear on your Vision and take daily action towards it. If you don't, your life and those you are meant to impact will suffer.

THE PATHWAY

Secret 13

Effective Goal-Setting

Goals establish the potential pathways from where you're currently at to where you want to go.

Coming to understand the importance of Mindset, Beliefs, and Vision transformed the way in which I saw myself, the world, and what was possible. However, as previously mentioned, my early attempts of setting Goals failed miserably. The core reason for this was simple: I didn't know *how* to effectively set Goals.

Like most people, I had vague ideas of what I wanted.

- I wanted to be a successful musician.
- I wanted to make a lot of money.
- I wanted to be healthy.
- I wanted to be happy.
- I wanted to be more intelligent.

The list went on.

But what do these even mean? These aren't Goals. They lack specificity. They lack detail. There's no way to measure them. They are basically useless. They are nice ideas, but useless.

Thanks to my friend and music marketing mentor, Danny Fournier of Oddball Productions, I was able to understand the flaws with my Goal-setting process and how to fix them. At this point, he was doing marketing and PR for my band.

We would often spend countless hours over coffee, discussing how I could take these massive dreams and ideas I had and condense them into realistic Goals; steps that I could actually begin to take. That was always my issue - big dreams, but no idea of how to get there. And no real starting point.

It was around this time that he put on a 10-week music marketing workshop for local artists and industry people. I was still working a minimum-wage job, still in debt, still trying to juggle everything in my life, and had very little free time. Frankly I was exhausted, mentally and physically. As a result, I was considering not going. I had many excuses not to.

However, I was desperate. At this point, it felt like a make or break situation. I couldn't fall back into old Habits, I couldn't just put it off until the 'perfect' moment arrived. Convenient or not, I needed to do whatever it took to make my dreams happen. I needed to capitalize on this opportunity. So with that in mind, I decided to go all in.

And I'm glad that I did - it changed the course of my life.

Asides from the incredible marketing value I received, which has become the Foundation for my knowledge today, it showed me why nothing I had desired up until that point had come to fruition. Though my Vision and Beliefs have fluctuated over the years, I've always had massive dreams and aspirations. The problem was that they were potential scenarios that could be 20 or 30 years down the road and not based on my current reality. I had no idea how I would get there. I was hopeful, but ignorant. It was wishful thinking at best.

Consequently, for years, I made no progress. There was a large gap between where I was and where I wanted to be. I always felt like I was waiting for the one perfect opportunity that would open up the pathway to my Goals. I always felt like I was waiting for the stars to align, or some special event to take place that would allow me to finally make progress. I was stuck and I had no idea how to begin walking the path.

I didn't know if I was working on the right things. I didn't know how to organize or prioritize tasks. I didn't know if I was making progress. I was lost. Because of this, I was always in a state of dreaming; of inaction, and any hope of achieving my dreams was fading away.

Remember how I said dreams are Goals without action? Well, I knew I needed to begin taking action. I needed to begin walking the path. Through Danny's mentorship and a lot of self-reflection, I came to understand how to effectively set and accomplish Goals. My life hasn't been the same since.

GOALS

Now that we have our Vision [Macro and Micro] outlined, we need to ensure we're able to take steps towards it. For many, it's easy to dream big but not take action - this is often our default. However, it's just as easy to get caught up in systems or processes that give us the illusion of making progress. Both approaches get us nowhere. Both approaches hold us back from our potential.

Therefore, balance is key.

The entire purpose of setting Goals is to help us achieve our Vision, this is why we must have our Vision clearly defined. Then, we need to effectively establish Goals that are most likely to get us there, based on our current knowledge. We then want to fall in love with the process of pursuing those Goals; testing, learning, exploring, and growing. Finally, if those Goals aren't getting us the results we desire, or we learn new things along the way, we need to make adjustments and modifications to continue our growth.

Through this process, we need to continually identify what's working and what's not so we can maximize output and minimize input. The quicker we can do this, the quicker we can continue to make progress and become the guitarists we've always dreamed of being.

Stay focused on the outcome, love the process, adapt when needed, and success is yours.

80/20 RULE

The 80/20 rule is also known as Pareto's Principle or more accurately as Pareto's Distribution. It is the notion that in many aspects of life and nature, 20% of cause often creates 80% of effect. This originally stemmed from economist Vilfredo Pareto's work, *Cours d'économie politique*, in which he outlined that approximately 80% of the land in Italy was owned by 20% of the population. There are varying degrees of this distribution, such as 75/25 or 90/10, but the idea is pretty consistent; there is a small percentage that creates a larger effect or has a larger influence.

When it comes to Goal-setting, this principle applies. There is so much information out there that might potentially help you achieve your Vision. However, it's far too easy to get lost in all of that information;

losing the forest for the trees. It gives the illusion of progress by focusing on the 'what' of learning - not the 'how' or 'why.' It keeps you busy, but as we know, being busy is *not* being productive.

So, as Practice Hackers, we need to be productive. We need to get the absolute most out of our practice sessions so we can become the guitarists we've always dreamed of being. This means with our Goals, we need to hyper-focus on the few tasks or skills that are most likely to create our desired result, for each area of our Micro Vision.

BRAINSTORM

For each of the 3 Fundamental Aspects of Guitar, list 5 potential skills that are most likely to help you achieve your Micro Vision for it. This means in total you will have 15 skills listed - 5 for each area. They can be skills that you currently know but want to improve, and/or that you don't know and want to learn. If there are more than 5 for each area, that's okay, just write out what comes to mind.

After you've done that with each area, you want to rank the skills in order from *most* likely to create the desired outcome [your Micro Vision], to *least* likely.

For example, if you have 5 skills listed, you want to rank them in order from 1-5 [1 being the most likely to create your desired outcome, 5 being the least likely].

S.M.A.R.T GOALS

S.M.A.R.T Goals were first discussed in the November 1981 issue of Management Review by George T. Doran. Though the concept has undergone different iterations, the overall idea is the same.

The way we're going to use this framework is as follows:

- **S** = Specific

- You want to create very specific Goals that are detailed and true to what you really want. If they are specific, they are more likely to be attained. They become more real.

- **M** = Measurable

  - Your Goals need to include a method of measurement so you actually gauge your progress. For guitar, here are some examples:

    - Tempo [BPM].

    - Clarity or precision [number of mistakes, percentage of accuracy].

    - The amount of a song, riff, or solo learned or created [percentage of completion].

- **A** = Achievable

  - Most people's Goals are too large or too vague and have no connection to reality. This is why it's key to create Goals that are achievable and realistic, and why I recommend starting with small, incremental Goals.

  - By doing this, you will gain what I call Achievement Momentum: small, consistent wins that reward you for the process and compound over time.

  - Achievement Momentum creates a positive association with pursuing your Goals. It gives you more confidence in your abilities, and it allows you to truly understand what you're capable of. It also helps you quickly form new Habits. As a result, you'll be able to make more progress, quicker, and it will be easier to set and accomplish larger Goals.

- **R** = Relevant

- This aligns with the 80/20 rule. You want to focus on what's relevant to your Vision - your outcome. You want to create Goals that are the most likely to create your desired result. Otherwise, you'll waste time, energy, and money.

- **T** = Time-bound

    - This is probably the most important part of setting your Goals.

    - There's something called Parkinson's Law which essentially describes the phenomena of how work expands to fill the time allotted. In other words, whether you have 1 hour or 10 hours to complete something, you'll find a way to use the time provided to complete it.

    - Timelines put pressure on us to take action. They allow us to push ourselves to make as much progress as we can, as quickly as we can. However, if we set Goals too far in the future, we'll be unlikely to actually attain them or make substantial progress.

    - This is why we want to work in smaller time frames, ideally in 8-week chunks as we'll discuss in **Secret 18**. Even if you have larger Goals that might take a year or more to complete, break them into 8-week chunks to begin working on them.

HOW TO CREATE S.M.A.R.T GOALS

By now, you should have already mapped out and ranked different skills that are most likely to create your desired result for each area of guitar [Technique, Theory, and Creativity].

The trick is to focus on a few skills, not many skills. We want to dedicate our time and resources to what will most likely create our desired result. Take the top 1-2 skills in each area that you outlined and focus on those:

- **Beginner:** 1 Goal for each area [3 Total]
- **Advanced:** 2 Goals for each area [6 Total]

These are the 20% that will create 80% of your results - your highest leverage Goals. When writing out Goals, I like to use empowering or encouraging language as well to help pre-program my mind's Beliefs around attaining it. In this way, they act as a sort of affirmation as well.

Take each skill and rewrite them as a S.M.A.R.T goal. Here's an example:

- **Skill:** Alternate picking
- **Goal:** I will easily alternate pick [insert piece of music or exercise] at 150bpm using 32nd notes with no mistakes by [insert date]

Some people would simply put 'I want to alternate pick faster' or 'I want to get better at guitar' for their Goals. Though these are better than nothing, they are vague and can't be measured. You don't actually know if you're making progress. S.M.A.R.T Goals allow for very specific targets to be established within different parameters that can be measured. You will know for a fact if you're making progress or not - but only if you're Tracking, which we discuss more in **Secret 18**.

RESOURCES

Personally, when I write out Goals, I also brainstorm different resources that might help me achieve them. They can be resources I'm already aware of, or even places I can look. Some examples might be books, courses, mentors, videos, articles, or other resources. This is where asking better questions or Making the Pinnacle of Others Your Foundation can really help.

3 POINTS OF PROGRESS

So now that we have S.M.A.R.T Goals established; the highest leverage steps towards our Vision, we want to identify what our Starting Points, Weak Points, and Checkpoints are along the way.

STARTING POINTS

- This is the Baseline. Whatever our Goal is, we want to identify where we are currently at with it.
- For Technique, this might be a certain speed that you can play comfortably at and correctly in relation to your Goal.
- For Theory, this might be the level of knowledge you have in relation to your Goal.
- For Creativity, this might be your ability to improvise or write in relation to your Goal.

WEAK POINTS

- Your Weak Points are discovered by pushing your Limits until you start making mistakes. These usually relate to your Performance Measurements as we discussed in **Secret 7**.
- We will discuss this a bit more in The Elite Framework, but the idea is that you're simply understanding where your Limits are, and what is potentially causing them.
- For example, with Technique, here are some Weak Points you might encounter as you're trying to build your speed:
  - Your hands are cramping.
  - Your hands aren't synchronizing.
  - You're playing the rhythm incorrectly.
  - You're playing the wrong notes or pitches.
  - You have difficulty switching between chords or parts.
  - Your pick is getting caught in the strings.
  - Your pinky is having trouble keeping up.
  - etc.

- Whatever the problem is, you want to identify it so you can work on it. This awareness allows us to focus our efforts on what's causing our issues, not wasting time and energy on what we're already good at.

- There is usually one main Weak Point that [if fixed] will help improve everything else [80/20]. This will likely come up repeatedly while using The Elite Framework, but it's good to understand it now so we have awareness prior to jumping into our practice routine.

CHECKPOINTS

- Having a timeline is critical to effective Goal-setting. But even with an 8-week Goal, it's easy to get caught up in the process, and you lose awareness of whether or not you're making progress. For this, it's important to establish Checkpoints along the way. These help enhance the effects of Parkinson's Law: you have the larger timeline, but now you also have smaller ones within it.

- You might set a Checkpoint at the halfway mark [4 weeks] or even bi-weekly or weekly. At the end of the day, find what works best for you to allow you to stay on track towards your Goals.

- However, note that progress isn't linear. You might set Checkpoints and fail to hit the first few, and then smash through the rest. Alternatively you might blast through the first Checkpoint and then struggle to continue that same progress.

- The idea with setting Checkpoints is simply to be aware of your progress as you're immersed in the process. They help break your Goals down into even more manageable chunks, which makes them easier to attain.

HOW TO APPLY THIS

The process of setting Goals doesn't need to be complicated. You simply need a system.

Now that you've identified your Micro Vision for each area of guitar [Technique, Theory, and Creativity]:

- Create a list of 5 skills that can help you achieve your Micro Vision for each area [15 total].

- Rank them based on which are most likely to create the desired outcome for each area [from 1-5].

- Convert the top 1-2 skills for each area into S.M.A.R.T Goals.

- Identify your Starting Point for each Goal.

- Identify your Weak Point for each Goal.

- Identify your Checkpoint(s) towards the completion of each Goal.

As you begin to accomplish your Goals, you'll come to better understand your Limits and your potential. This will aid you in setting more accurate Goals. Don't get overwhelmed or think everything has to be absolutely perfect right now. Start with what you have. Then, after the 8-week program, revisit and adjust. This is the best way to learn - by doing. So get started.

Practice Hacker Tip: Create highly-effective Goals by following the S.M.A.R.T framework and by focusing on the 80/20 rule.

BOOK III

THE ELITE FRAMEWORK FOR PRACTICING LIKE A PRO AND SKYROCKETING PROGRESS

ELITE PROGRAM DESIGN

Secret 14

Daily Routine and Weekly Sequencing

Regardless of your Routine or Sequencing, optimize your use of The Elite Framework within 10-minute Practice Sprints, taking an Effective Break in-between them.

Most people are reactionary to life. Since birth they have become a product of circumstance, instead of a producer of it. In other words, the chaos of the external world becomes the chaos of their internal world. This shapes their Beliefs, informs their Vision, and creates the blueprint in which their entire life is built from.

We have countless responsibilities that require our attention daily; work, school, family, friends, relationships, chores, and everything in-between. All of our time and energy gets caught up in what the world requires from us. As a result, what we desire out of life often gets put on hold. We get stuck. This becomes increasingly difficult to manage when deep down you aspire for something more. You have ambitions, desires, hopes, and dreams all showing you what's possible, yet you aren't able to pursue them. Or so you think.

We believe there is something noble in self-sacrifice. Most of us will put everyone and everything above our own wants and needs. The problem is that by not taking care of yourself first; by not making time for what's important to you, and what fulfills you - you're actually causing harm to yourself and to others. You're not becoming the person you're capable of being. You're not becoming more. Everyone suffers.

This was me, and I'm sure you've been here as well, if you aren't right now. Life was always pulling at me, I felt like I had no control, but deep down, I knew that I needed to escape. I needed to regain control. I needed to begin the pathway towards my destiny. I just didn't know where to start.

The issue was that I never seemed to have enough time. Something always required my attention and focus. I felt stuck. Not just a bit uncomfortable, but *stuck*. No time, no money, in debt - stuck.

So if I couldn't find *more* time, then I had to understand how I could maximize the time I did have. I didn't think I was inefficient with my time. I always felt busy; jumping between different tasks, feeling like I was juggling the world. Yet, I wasn't producing any results. I was driving myself into insanity. I learned the hard way that being busy and being productive are two entirely different things. Upon further reflection, I came to understand what I needed to address. If I was to make any progress on guitar or in life, I needed to maximize output and minimize input.

Relating to the 80/20 rule, it was critical that I simplified the tasks that I was doing. Whatever it was, I needed to focus on the few factors that were most likely to produce my desired outcome. This was difficult at first because I was so caught up in my 'to-do list.' I had what seemed like hundreds of tasks to do, but never enough time to do them. I gave them all equal importance.

So with guitar, if I had little time to practice, I couldn't focus on 10 different areas at once. I had to focus on what was most likely going to help me achieve my Vision. But just applying this to my Goals wasn't enough. If I was going to do this, I had to figure out how to extract the most benefit from the smallest period of time. I had to focus purely on what created results, and I had to discard anything that wasted time. This is where I knew that I needed a new approach, and I took Inspiration from the fitness world.

Often, people do cardio to lose fat, and lift weights to put on muscle, but there is one form of working out that often does both. More importantly, it focuses on pure effectiveness and efficiency: interval training. This can be done with cardio or even with circuit training, it doesn't really matter. In most cases, you can have a 10-20-minute session, alternating between periods of work and periods of rest, and get incredible results.

If I was going to get elite-level results on guitar without needing to practice all day, I had to maximize my sessions in a similar way. Whereas most practice sessions barely touch the Skill Development Zone [where progress actually happens], I knew that my entire session needed to revolve around it. If my practice session was too short, I wouldn't hit it. If it was too long, I would waste time and energy.

We need to maximize the output of a session [results] and minimize the input [time and excess energy]. Think of sprinting. If you sprint once, you won't benefit a lot. If you try sprinting for 2-3 minutes straight, you'll burn out, risk hurting yourself, and you probably only benefited from the first 20-30 seconds anyways. However, if you sprint within a small period of time, then you can optimize your performance. You can perfect each stride, you can continually push your Limits in a controlled manner, and once you adapt - you can add modifications to continue your growth.

So, to get the absolute most out of our guitar practice sessions, we must work in 'Practice Sprints.' During these Sprints, we want to use The Elite

Framework to constantly push the Skill Development Zone. By doing this, we suddenly go from engaging the Skill Development Zone for, on average, 3-6 minutes per 60-minute session, to engaging it for the *entire* 60-minute session. This alone increases the results of *each session* by 10-20x. Just imagine how much progress you'll make and how much opportunity will open up for you.

The Old Framework barely touches the Skill Development Zone. It's no wonder that it takes months and years to make progress using it. It's no wonder why so many guitarists give up or fail to reach their potential. For so long we have made guitar practice way more complicated than it has to be. We've always focused on *what* we're practicing, yet we've never really focused on *how* or *why*.

There *is* a way to master the art of practice. There *is* a way to become the guitarist you've always dreamed of being without needing to practice all day. And one of the key ways to do this, is by practicing in controlled Sprints.

The goal of working in Sprints is to optimize every second within them, extracting as much benefit as we possibly can. Then, once we stop making progress, we simply add in Practice Variables [as we'll discuss in **Secret 18**] to continue growing. The beautiful thing about The Elite Framework is that it's designed in a way that constantly pushes Limits, addresses issues, fixes them, and then pushes new Limits. As a result, adaptation occurs at a much slower rate. However, when it does, we have ways to overcome it and we can continue to break through. Nothing can stop you now.

DAILY ROUTINE TYPES

There are many routine types, but what matters is consistency. You want to start with a simpler routine to get used to the processes we are describing throughout this book, develop the Habit, and truly understand your Limits so you can effectively push them. Start with the basics; remember

Pinnacle/Foundation Theory. Then you can adjust when needed as you adapt and require more stimulus to grow.

Because there are 3 main areas of practice, I've established 3 main routine types. They all fit within a 1-hour practice session of *actual work*. If you absolutely cannot dedicate 1 hour to practicing each day, you can cut all of these values in half. However, for best results, I highly recommend finding a way to practice for at least 1 hour a day.

1-DAY PRACTICE ROUTINE OUTLINE

- **Level:** Beginner
- **Goals Per Area:** 1
- This is primarily for beginners but I recommend that everyone starts here. This will become your Foundation. This is also ideal if you're focusing on 1 Goal per each area of practice.
- This 1-Day Practice Routine goes through all 3 areas of practice [Technique, Theory, and Creativity] in 1 session.
- Each area receives 20 minutes total to work on your Goal, which you will approach in Practice Sprints of 10 minutes, separated by an Effective Break [described later in this chapter].

2-DAY PRACTICE ROUTINE OUTLINE

- **Level:** Intermediate or Lagging
- **Goals Per Area:** 2
- In your Micro Vision, you ranked each area of practice [Technique, Theory, and Creativity] out of 10. This routine is ideal if you have a lagging area you want to improve and you have 2 Goals to work on for each area.
- This 2-Day Practice Routine repeats the lagging area over both days, whereas the other areas fall on either day. This means that over 2 days, you're working on 1 area twice, and 2 areas once.

- Each session focuses on 2 areas, each being given 30 minutes to work on. Each area will have 2 Goals to work on in 15-minute Practice Sprints, divided by an Effective Break.

3-DAY PRACTICE ROUTINE OUTLINE

- **Level:** Advanced
- **Goals Per Area:** 2+
- This is ideal for individuals who have optimized the other routines and extracted as much benefit as possible from them, including using Practice Variables to overcome plateaus.
- This 3-Day Practice Routine focuses on 1 area per day.
- Each session focuses on 2 Goals per area, providing 30 minutes for each
- Depending on your strategy and needs, you can work in 10, 15, or even 30-minute Practice Sprints, divided by Effective Breaks.
- As you become more advanced, you'll understand how many Goals you can work on effectively at one time and how to properly push yourself. Adjust and customize as needed if you're at this level.

So, now that we understand the overall approach of the 1, 2, and 3-Day Routines, what might this actually look like?

DAILY ROUTINE EXAMPLES

1-DAY PRACTICE ROUTINE EXAMPLE [Beginner: 1 Goal for Each Area]

- **Technique:** 20min Alternate Picking
- **Theory:** 20min Triads
- **Creativity:** 20min Songwriting

For each area, you'll focus on 1 Goal. You'll start with a 10-minute Practice Sprint, followed by an Effective Break, followed by another 10-minute Practice Sprint. Then you'll go onto the next area.

2-DAY PRACTICE ROUTINE EXAMPLE [Intermediate: 2 Goals for Each Area, or Lagging]

- **Technique:** 15min Alternate Picking + 15min Economy Picking
- **Theory:** 15min Triads + 15min Modes
- **Creativity:** 15min Songwriting + 15min Improvisation

For each area, you'll focus on 2 Goals. The first Goal will be a 15-minute Sprint, followed by an Effective Break. You'll repeat this for the second Goal, then you'll go onto the next area.

3-DAY PRACTICE ROUTINE EXAMPLE [Advanced: 2+ Goals for Each Area, More Physical and Mental Demand]

- **Technique:** 30min Alternate Picking + 30min Economy Picking
- **Theory:** 30min Triads + 30min Modes
- **Creativity:** 30min Songwriting + 30min Improvisation

For each area, you'll focus on 2 Goals. The first Goal will start with a 15-minute Sprint, divided by an Effective Break, followed by another 15-minute Sprint. You'll repeat this for the second goal, then you'll go onto the next area.

Remember, when possible you want to engage the Compounding Effect. If you're practicing skills that are too far removed from each other, it might be difficult to enter into a state of Productivity. So ensure you're combining similar skills or ones that connect to each other if taking on multiple Goals.

This is something you'll need to become more aware of and is another part of developing your self-regulation abilities. These routines are simply examples to help you develop your Foundation with this New Framework. There is no one-size-fits-all approach. Keep that in mind.

ROUTINE TYPE TO START WITH

I recommend that everyone starts with the 1-Day Practice Routine. Even if you're more advanced, there are a lot of new concepts in this book and it's critical that you properly learn and integrate them. Start simple, integrate, then expand.

Once you've maximized what you're capable of doing with the 1-Day Practice Routine, including using the Practice Variables that we'll discuss in **Secret 18**, then you can move onto the other routines, or further customize your own.

WEEKLY SEQUENCING

So now that we have an idea of the different routine types, how do they get organized throughout the week? Good question! Each routine type is spread out across the week differently. Essentially, after every period of work, there's rest.

- 1-Day Routine: 1 Day of Practice, 1 Day of Rest, Repeat
- 2-Day Routine: 2 Days of Practice, 1 Day of Rest, Repeat
- 3-Day Routine: 3 Days of Practice, 1 Day of Rest, Repeat

As you become more advanced, you can experiment with just repeating practice daily until you stop getting results, or you can mix up the days and approaches. But again, start with the basic routine and sequencing until you extract as much as you can from it, then move on.

FREE PLAY

As you know by now, there's a lot of intense information in this book. It's really focused around optimization, efficiency, and making serious progress. But what about just having fun with guitar? Isn't that the whole point?

At least once a week, with any of these sequences, there is a recommended day of Free Play. Think of it like a 'cheat day' if you will - just do whatever you want, have fun, forget the rules. This doesn't mean that you can't Free Play any other time, it's just that it dedicates an entire day or practice session to it in case you're limited on time and you want to ensure you get your practice sessions in.

For the 1 and 2-Day Routines, you can throw in a Free Play day on Sunday or another day of the week that works best for you. For the 3-Day Routine, the days alternate a bit differently but throw in a Free Play day as needed.

WEEKLY SEQUENCING EXAMPLES

LEGEND:

- P = Practice
- R = Rest
- F = Free Play

1-DAY ROUTINE [MON-SUN]:

- P R P R P R F

2-DAY ROUTINE [MON-SUN]:

- P P R P P R F

3-DAY ROUTINE [MON-SUN]:

- Week 1: P P P R P P P

- Week 2: R P P P R P P
- Week 3: P R P P P R P
- Week 4: P P R P P P R
- As you can see, this doesn't quite fit into the weekly system. This approach offers 3 days of practice with 1 day of rest, and that cycle repeats. Add a Free Play day as needed.

Again, these are just some examples of how you can arrange your practice sessions throughout the week. Find what works for you. Find what allows you to be consistent. Start with the basics, build your Foundation, and go from there. Don't overcomplicate it.

EFFECTIVE BREAK

WHAT IS IT

Similar to interval training - after a period of full capacity work [Practice Sprint], we need to rest. However, we aren't just stopping - we want to switch up the stimulation to encourage the body and mind to reset.

Here are some examples:

- Washing your face with cold water.
- Physical Exercise [jogging, jumping jacks, push-ups, sprinting, etc.].
- Reading or listening to something that inspires you or shifts your focus temporarily.

WORK-TO-REST RATIO

Start with 10-minute Practice Sprints. If you can't push your Sprint to 10 minutes, start with 5 or 7. Divide each Sprint with a 1 to 2-minute Effective Break.

Remember, this is like interval training, so optimize for the given timeframe to ensure you're doing the correct work at full capacity and extracting as much benefit as possible. Then, once you hit a Limit [reach adaptation], you can modify as needed with the information you'll learn in **Secret 18**.

HOW TO APPLY THIS

Start with the 1-Day Routine and Weekly Sequencing, focusing on 1 Goal per area of guitar. You will follow this for the entire 8-week program.

To get the most out of our practice sessions we need to optimize every second of them so we're constantly engaging the Skill Development Zone. This means we need to work in Practice Sprints to ensure we're pushing at full capacity within small, controlled periods of time. This way, we're not overworking ourselves, and we can be consistent with *how* we practice as well as *how often* we practice.

Once adaptation is hit, we can then add in different Practice Variables to continue our growth, as we will discuss in **Secret 18**.

> **Practice Hacker Tip:** Maximize output while minimizing input by utilizing Practice Sprints divided by Effective Breaks to continually push the Skill Development Zone. This is where the elites play.

Secret 15

Pillars of Consistency

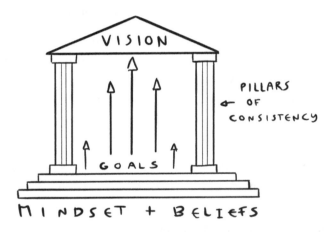

The Pillars of Consistency build the temple. There are 2 core Pillars of Consistency: Habit & Motivation.

One of the most difficult tasks for humans is changing our behaviour - at least willingly. Think of how some people, even when confronted with new information, refuse to change because 'that's just how they are.' Think of the ways that you act around certain people, the way you approach your life, the actions you take [or don't take]. These are all different behaviours which stem from your Mindset and Beliefs [whether conscious or unconscious].

It wasn't until I started trying to turn my life around that I realized how difficult it was to actually change behaviours. For so long I had always put that process off. I would tell myself lies like 'I don't actually want to do that' or 'that's just not who I am.' Yet, these were simply just excuses. I was protecting my ego. I was lazy. I was complacent.

Because of this, it actually created a lot of internal tension. I was starting to understand what I had to do to create the results I wanted in life. However, it felt nearly impossible to get myself to commit, at least consistently. I knew deep down that I wanted to change. I wanted to set Goals and begin chipping away at them. I wanted to create a morning routine. I wanted to develop healthier Habits. I wanted to do all of these things, yet it seemed like nothing was able to stick. I often found myself falling into old Habits by default.

I'm sure you can relate to this. Think of all the things you 'wish' you could do, or 'know' you should do - yet there isn't enough Motivation or drive to make them happen. You're not able to create the new Habit. Instead, you resort to your 'default' way of acting and behaving. You resort to 'comfort.'

The issue with changing our routine and trying something new, is the association we make with the change. There's comfort in what we know and discomfort in what we don't. This is a natural, protective mechanism, but often fails to serve us in the ways that we need in the modern world.

PILLAR I: HABIT

IMPORTANCE

We are creatures of Habit - yet we aren't always in control of the Habits we form. They form both consciously and unconsciously as a result of our Beliefs, our behaviours, and consequently, our actions. As we gain deeper self-awareness, we are able to more actively engage with our own evolution. We begin to take control of our lives; of our destiny. So it's clear that we need to establish Habits and routines that serve our Beliefs, Vision, and Goals. We need to be congruent. We need to be consistent.

By developing Habits, we create new associations to replace old ones. As we immerse ourselves in the process, rewards [Goals] will happen as a result. We just need to make sure that our daily action is calibrated towards our Vision and that we are making adjustments as we go. This is why it's so important to fall in love with the process of pursuing a Goal; the process of becoming more. It takes a lot to leave your place of comfort and pull through the inevitable struggle you'll face along your pathway to success. This is why many never accomplish greatness - they are too afraid to begin. If you're strictly focused on the outcome, it might not be enough Motivation to pull you through the process to get there. Even worse, you'll continue to reinforce a negative association with the pursuit of your Goals and you'll further enforce a positive association with comfort.

As the saying goes: comfort kills success - but it doesn't stop there. Comfort breeds procrastination, which means you'll not only struggle to succeed, but you'll also struggle to start. If you follow this path, you'll live in a perpetual state of hoping and dreaming, yet your life will never change. In your last moments, you'll still be left wondering what could've been - not what was.

I keep bringing this up because it's absolutely critical to your success on guitar, and in life. The world's greatest musicians and performers didn't just wake up one day immensely talented. They had Empowering Beliefs, they had a Vision, they set Goals, and they did whatever it took to achieve them. This means they weren't just lazy and unmotivated, or just 'lucky.' There are always exceptions, but they are never the rule.

These people developed the Habits required to produce the results they desired, even if they didn't always want to. They learned to immerse themselves in the process of becoming more. Their 'why' was big enough to pull them through the struggle. Their 'why' was big enough to get them started.

Many successful people will tell you a similar story: Winning is Beginning.

So, if you're living in a prison of comfort, procrastination, and excuses - you aren't able to begin. If you aren't able to begin, you'll never win. And everyone suffers.

Listen, I get it. We always want to put our best foot forward - especially as musicians. We wear our hearts on our sleeves and our craft is the fullest expression of who we are. We *have* to get it right. People *need* to understand us. The issue though, is those who procrastinate always wait for the perfect moment and that moment never comes. Perfectionism becomes an excuse for procrastination and ultimately laziness. There's comfort in the known, but discomfort in the unknown. It holds them back from living the life they are meant to live, and having the impact they are meant to have. It holds them back from beginning.

You may have a strong set of Beliefs and even have Goals laid out, but if you desire to achieve your Vision - the Pillars of Consistency build the temple. The temple is you - your potential, your purpose, your path, your destiny.

Think of it like this. What is more effective:

- Going on a fad diet once a year to lose weight and 'get healthy?' Building it up to be a massive, uncomfortable event that requires a lot of your time, focus, and energy preparing for? Then after you're done, you simply fall back into old Habits - enforcing your negative association with exercise, weight loss, and the pursuit of health.
- Or, losing weight and 'getting healthy' by taking small, consistent steps, and creating a lifestyle around it? Enforcing positive associations with the process, establishing new Foundations, and experiencing results as the reward of Consistency?

I'll give you a hint: it's not the first scenario.

Yet that's how so many people approach building a Habit, especially as it relates to learning or improving a skill. They make it out to be a monumental change, and as a result they often lose before they can begin.

You need to build a lifestyle that supports your Beliefs, Vision, and Goals. You need to become immersed in the process - it needs to become a part of who you are. Then success becomes a reward of the journey, not the sole focus. This is what allows for consistency.

Through building the Pillars of Consistency, you'll internalize this new Habit; automating it, developing it, and expanding off of it. Another example of Pinnacle/Foundation Theory in action.

The key to developing a Habit is to start. Make small changes, create incremental Goals. Whatever it is, start small, but start. Winning is Beginning.

HOW LONG DOES IT TAKE TO FORM A HABIT?

Typically, a Habit can take anywhere from 21-66+ days to form. However, it's less about the time involved and more about the strength of the physical, mental, and emotional connections you're making as you're developing the Habit. By engaging with the principles outlined in this book, Habit formation will happen much quicker because many different levels of learning are being engaged.

Keep in mind that by taking the time to form a Habit, it will establish positive associations with the process, which will allow you to stick with the Habit, dive deeper into it, and extract more out of it. So even if you struggle at first, knowing what we know about learning and developing new skills, the same can apply to Habits. The more we do it, and the better we do it - the stronger the Habit, and the quicker it will form, naturally. This knowledge alone might help you be consistent enough to build the Habit, create the lifestyle, and begin reaping the rewards.

EMOTIONAL STATE

I believe the biggest factor in developing a Habit is the degree in which you're emotionally connected to it. By discovering how the new Habit can improve multiple areas of your life, it can establish the positive associations needed to prioritize the Habit, and stick with it long enough to actually see results.

For example:

- Guitar practice on its own doesn't mean a lot to most people. It's not a priority. It's something we know we 'should' do, but it's simply another bullet point on our ever-expanding 'to-do' list. It's something we will get to once everything else gets done. This representation is 1-dimensional and very limiting. In this context, it's a low-leverage task.

- However, for the Practice Hacker, this changes. We recognize the journey towards mastering guitar as a reflection of our journey towards mastering life. By engaging with the principles within this book, we are taking control of our musical destinies. But it doesn't stop there. We see this transformation as a microcosm of a larger transformation happening in our lives. It might start with guitar, but it doesn't end with guitar. These principles can apply to every area of life. The deeper we engage with them, it will not only allow us to become the guitarists we've always dreamed of being, but it will also allow us to become the people we've always dreamed of being; becoming our potential, becoming more.

See how this change in perspective has brought more excitement and importance to the idea of guitar practice? That by embracing these principles and frameworks, you are actually improving all areas of your life, even who you are as a person? Makes it a bit easier to prioritize, wouldn't you agree? Guitar practice is now a high-leverage task. In fact, a *very* high-leverage task.

Also, as you begin experiencing small wins during the development of your Habit, you'll associate positive emotions with doing it, and negative emotions with not doing it. You'll be rewarded for the process, and as a result, you'll fall in love with it. This will develop the awareness, Beliefs, and confidence needed to accomplish even bigger Goals. This is why it's so important to properly set Goals following the system we discussed in **Secret 13**. It allows you to more easily gain Achievement Momentum, which will aid you in forming the Habit and creating the lifestyle you need to support your Beliefs, Vision, and Goals.

INCENTIVE

We are creatures of Habit, but also reward. This can get us into trouble, but if we're in control, we can use it to our advantage. Just like you might treat yourself with a 'cheat day' once a week on the journey towards your fitness Goals, you want to incentivize the formation of your Habit with guitar practice. You might not need to incentivize yourself for a long time, but until you're able to create the Habit and fall in love with the process, consider treating yourself. Maybe this is after a full week of consistent practice. Maybe it's after you hit a Checkpoint or a smaller Goal.

The treat can be something as simple as an ice-cream, a fun meal, a visit to your favourite place or store, a movie, or anything else that you love but don't get to do often. It doesn't have to be complicated, extravagant, or even cost money. The idea is to find some way to convince and encourage your mind to stick with the new Habit, even if you're having an off day or you lack the Motivation. Habits are easy to develop when life is easy. However, life isn't always easy. When it becomes difficult, that's when it's most important to stick with and develop the Habit. Consistency becomes the anchor that keeps us grounded even in the most turbulent waters. So find a way, big or small, or pull you through to your end-goal; your Vision. It's worth it, trust me.

At first, rewarding yourself might be necessary. However, as you develop the Habit and start to create positive associations with the process, the experience of pursuing your Goals and becoming more will often be all the incentive you need.

Again, this is similar to fitness. You might initially be incentivized by the result that you want, which is great, but after a week of hard effort and suffering, if you're not seeing substantial progress it becomes very difficult to stick with it. However, if you find a way to incentivize yourself to stay on track [weekly cheat days, or maybe buying yourself something as a reward] then you'll develop the Habit a lot easier. Through that Habit, you'll learn to love the process of working out, eating healthy, and pushing yourself. It will be less about the end-goal, but more about the process. You'll love every small step you take, and each Checkpoint or milestone you hit. Every day will feel like a Goal is being accomplished simply by engaging with this new Habit.

It becomes a lifestyle. Then when you don't work out, or don't eat well, you have a negative association with it, which will help keep you on track. By focusing on the process, you'll be rewarded with accomplishing your Goals. This allows you to sustain your Habit much easier.

This is where we want to get with any Habit, but especially with guitar. Make the Habit of achieving your Goals a part of your daily routine - fall in love with the process of becoming more. It will support your pathway towards your dreams, and as you begin seeing results, you'll never want to stop! Practice Hacking is a lifestyle. Time to develop the Habit.

MORNING ROUTINE

One of the easiest ways to develop a Habit, is by placing it into your morning routine. Maybe it's after your shower, after your morning coffee, or right before breakfast. Whatever it is, if you're struggling to create a new Habit, make it central to your morning routine. This will allow you to engage the new Habit at the same time every day, as well as in the same environment, with far greater control of your circumstances and the potential variables. All of this optimizes your Productivity as well, as discussed in **Secret 10**.

The time we have in the morning is usually the only time we have to ourselves before the world begins making demands of us. Take that time to develop yourself and focus on your highest-leverage tasks [in this case, guitar practice]. Then, no matter what else happens that day, you're making progress towards your Vision; you're in control; you win.

We will discuss this more in **Secrets 16** and **18** but routines allow you to more easily access your Ideal State; your state of maximum resourcefulness and Productivity. By creating a better morning routine, especially one that includes guitar practice, you're not only immersing yourself in the process of accomplishing your Goals, but you're also setting up your entire day for success. You'll be in your Ideal State. You'll be able to react to situations with more clarity. You'll have more energy. You'll have greater perspective. You'll be in a better mood. You'll have more excitement and drive. You'll be in control of your state.

This is being proactive. This is how you win. This is the way of the Practice Hacker.

PILLAR II: MOTIVATION

POSITIVE PULL, NEGATIVE PUSH

Vision cannot be attained without Consistency. Habit is a critical Pillar of Consistency, but it cannot operate alone. One of the biggest reasons people don't build towards their Goals is because they don't have the Pillar of Motivation.

We can't always control what happens to us. The same goes for relying on states like Motivation, Productivity, or Creativity. If it's already there, then we should capitalize on it, but a true Practice Hacker cultivates it at will. This is what separates us from the rest. We are proactive. We control how we react. We control our state.

If you've been following along, you've outlined your Vision as a guitarist. You've identified the best-case scenario for your life if you pursue your

Goals. This can often be enough Motivation to help you stay on track. However, we know that with the pursuit of anything worthwhile, there is the inevitability of suffering. If you're developing a new Habit, it's going to be outside of your comfort zone. Because of this, your brain is going to seek comfort [where you're currently at, what's familiar] and will push you away from discomfort [where you want to be, what's unfamiliar]. The more you make a new Habit out to be a monumental event or change, the worse this situation will be, and the less likely you'll be able to ever achieve your Vision.

So how do you fix this? Simply put, we need to associate enough pleasure with developing the Habit, and enough pain with not developing it, to keep us in check. This is where reflecting on your worst-case scenario comes into play.

As mentioned before, I'm a firm believer that everyone has a unique role to play in this world. Everyone has a unique purpose, no matter how 'big' or 'small.' Self-awareness is the first step to this realization. Once you become aware that you're not where you want to be in life, and that there is something more for you out there, it's similar to taking the **Red Pill** in the Matrix. You can't go back. You're now actively engaging with your own path and evolution. You're using your eyes for the first time. Every action has a consequence.

You have a choice to make:

- Do you take on the journey of building towards your potential? Towards greater perfection? Immersing yourself in the process of becoming more? Cultivating the person you need to be in order to create the Vision you hold for yourself, and for all of those you're meant to impact?

- Or do you waste away your potential due to apathy or laziness? Living a life of regret? Leaving a void in the world just as big as the unique hole you were meant to fill, everyone suffering as a result? All because you couldn't be bothered to get a little uncomfortable?

If you need to, print out your Vision [best-case and worst-case scenario] and post it on your wall or somewhere you will see it often. Whatever it takes. Remind yourself daily of your potential; of what you genuinely desire, of who you want to be. And remind yourself of what happens if you give up.

Remember, as a guitarist, you have a very unique and amazing gift. Whether you want to be a rockstar, you want to learn your favourite songs, you want to be a guitar teacher, or anything in-between - *you* hold the incredible power of music in your hands. Whatever you choose to do with it is up to you, but many people would give anything to be in the position you're in. Don't take it for granted. Learn more. Become more. And make the world a better place as a result.

VISUALIZATION

Though you can engage physical tasks to develop a Habit [which we will discuss more in **Secret 16**], Habits are ultimately formed in your mind. Your brain interprets experiences internally and externally in very similar ways - there are just varying degrees of intensity. These affect the impact of the experience and the formation of its memory.

As outlined in Tony Robbins' book, *Unlimited Power*, you often have certain mental imagery representative of certain states. Even your physiology changes. Your breathing changes. Effectively, *you* change depending on your thoughts/emotions, and this dictates how you act in the world around you.

By understanding what type of mental imagery and emotional state you experience when you're motivated, you can apply those same qualities to a state in which you're unmotivated - reprogramming your mind.

For example:

- Think of when you were last strongly motivated to do something - picture it. Notice the brightness and colours of the image. What emotions does it evoke? Usually, with more positive, motivated states, they hold powerful imagery that appears as bright, colourful, sharp, large, in focus, and other similar qualities. What is your breathing like? What effect does this state have on your physiology? Note everything you can.

- However, when we are unmotivated, it is often a very different mental image. Try visualizing something you're unmotivated to do. How does it look or feel? Dim? Colourless? Sad? Bleak? Boring? Hopeless? What is your breathing like? What effect does this state have on your physiology? Note everything you can.

- Try shifting that unmotivated image into one with the qualities of the motivated image. Replace the old with the new. Make it brighter, larger, more colourful - whatever the qualities are. You need to be as accurate as possible. The more accurate you are in shifting the unmotivated image into the qualities of the motivated image, the better the connection will be - therefore the result.

- Encode this through perfected repetition [3-7 times in a row should be fine, but add more if needed]. This will establish new associations in your mind, changing that previously unmotivated image into a motivated image; changing your state, changing your behaviour, and changing your actions.

- You can do this for any type of state you wish to change - it's simply a matter of identifying the preferred mental imagery, transforming the undesired imagery, and creating and strengthening these new connections and associations. You're programming your mind to serve your needs.

For most of us, this mental imagery is formed as a response to our environment. This process has served us in the past, but we've never really been in control of it. We've been reactionary. As awareness removes mystery, now that we understand the mechanisms at play, we need to gain control and develop them in a way that best serves our needs. We need to be proactive.

By identifying old mental imagery that no longer serves us, and creating new mental imagery in its place, we are reprogramming our mind to support our Beliefs, Vision, and Goals.

ACCOUNTABILITY

Sometimes, even with the best of intentions, it's difficult to move outside of your comfort zone - especially when the onus is on you. It's easy to choose comfort over the unknown. Who is going to know anyways?

We often prioritize work, school, or other responsibilities because we 'have' to do them. Well why do we 'have' to do them? Primarily, it's because other people rely on us; they hold us accountable. There are rewards for success and consistency, but more importantly - there are real consequences for failure and inconsistency.

If you're struggling to develop a new Habit, consider finding an accountability partner - someone to hold your feet to the fire, someone to help keep you on track. You might only need their help early on, but it's one of the best ways to gain Motivation and establish a new Habit.

Consider setting a 'punishment' for yourself if you don't meet your Goals. Your accountability partner will help enforce it. Some examples are:

- Shaving your head, dying your hair an awful colour, or getting an outrageous haircut.
- Going out in public with an embarrassing outfit or sign on.
- Donating to a political party or cause that you dislike [give the money or check to your accountability partner, and if you don't achieve your Goals, they donate it].

I'm sure many more ideas are running through your mind.

Find what works best for you. The greater the negative association with the punishment, the more likely you'll see your Goals through. Your Motivation now exists outside of your own mind and has real-world consequences - there is much more at stake.

Additionally, social media can be a great tool for accountability. By publicly announcing your Goals, you're putting yourself on display for the whole world to see. If you succeed, people will look up to you, be inspired, and will cheer you on. If you fail because you gave up or got lazy, people are going to see you in a much different light.

So, if you're struggling with finding Motivation or building a Habit - up the stakes, find an accountability partner, and make the consequences real.

HOW TO APPLY THIS

So now we understand that the Pillars of Consistency build the temple. The temple is you - your potential, your purpose, your path, your destiny. The Foundation of that temple is your Mindset and Beliefs.

To make the process of achieving your Goals a lifestyle, you must form a Habit and cultivate Motivation at will. There are many strategies to do this - explore them all, find what works best, and refine its use. Don't overcomplicate it.

Make it easy to get started. Incentivize yourself early on to form the Habit of guitar practice. Remind yourself of your Vision and what will happen if you don't pursue it. Don't make the formation of your new Habit out to be bigger than it is. The more you put it on a pedestal, the less likely you'll be to succeed.

Our goal is to fall in love with the process of becoming more, gaining Achievement Momentum, forming a Habit and establishing a new lifestyle. As a result, success will be rewarded as a part of the journey, not the end-goal or sole focus.

Your communication with yourself programs your mind. The more in control you are of this process, the greater power you have over your own life.

And if you really need the extra boost, consider finding an accountability partner to hold your feet to the fire, or even make your Goals public.

All of this is to help you develop a set of tools to understand your limitations and ways that help you overcome them. If you find other ways that work, and allow you to be consistent - use them. Whatever it takes to cultivate Motivation, form the Habit, and immerse yourself in the process of practice. Whatever it takes to unlock your potential and become more.

> **Practice Hacker Tip:** Your ability to build the Pillars of Consistency directly correlates with the degree of your success.

THE PRACTICE ROUTINE

Secret 16

Ideal State [Synergy]: Preparing for Practice

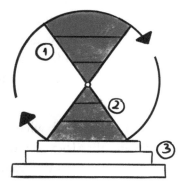

Cultivate your highest state of resourcefulness and potential through achieving Ideal State [Synergy].

Following the Old Framework, my results were dramatically inconsistent. I was always hoping for the best, but my playing felt out of my control. Some days I would play terribly, while other days I would feel like a rockstar. I just assumed that's how being a musician was. I was reactionary.

I thought that I was experiencing this problem because I wasn't practicing enough. That if I just put more time in, everything would sort itself out. Eventually, I would have the Foundation needed to jump on stage or enter the studio and be 'ready to go.'

However, I was wrong. This wasn't a smart approach, and honestly, it only caused me pain and suffering. It was frustrating to feel so out of control with my own abilities. I can't even count the number of times I would nail a part in my bedroom, then I'd get on stage and it's like I forgot how to play. Or I would be in the studio and unable to play the simplest of riffs. I wasn't in control. I wasn't able to be at my best. As a result, every area of my life suffered.

Throughout this book, I've spoken about my experiences with hitting a wall of progress - in guitar, and in life. I wasn't able to move forward. It was a very testing time. For a moment, I truly experienced a sense of hopelessness. As you know by now, this led me to seek out the world's best guitarists, musicians, and performers to see what they were doing that I wasn't; what set them apart from the average. It couldn't just be 'chance' or 'luck.' It couldn't just be some 'gift' or 'talent.' These people were highly successful and had a lot riding on their ability to perform well - they *had* to be in control. Their careers, and their lives depended on it.

In the pursuit of answers, I discovered what set them apart - their framework. They think differently. They act differently. They see life differently. And, because of this, they get different results.

However, there was something more to this. Something I hadn't previously considered. Something that was so obvious, yet I had completely overlooked. It wasn't until I read *Unlimited Power* by Tony Robbins that it all came into focus. The answer: Anchoring.

Many of the most successful individuals in the world use some sort of routine or ritual to put them into their peak state; their highest level of resourcefulness. This gives them control over their abilities, allowing for optimal performance. But for the best of the best, they take this a step further. They establish Anchors which trigger their peak state on command, without needing complicated routines or rituals to get there.

So, to get the most out of The Elite Framework, and to become the guitarists we've always dreamed of being, it requires that we master our ability to access our peak state at will - which for us is our Ideal State [Synergy]. This primes our mind and body to maximize our results in the smallest amount of time. It also requires that we master the other Practice Secrets of the Pros. The deeper you integrate this information and build off of it, the greater the results you will have. Your pathway to mastery is limited by your ability to make these concepts your Foundation.

#1 IDEAL STATE [MENTAL]

Think of those moments where you just felt everything 'click.' Where you were learning or playing something and you felt energized, electric, and almost superhuman. Everything was working perfectly. Your playing was locked in, everything was fluid. You were inspired, you were creative. It probably even felt surreal or transcendental in some way, like you were playing far beyond your normal ability. This is often referred to as your peak state or flow state, but it goes even deeper. It's what I'll refer to as your Ideal State [Mental].

The problem is that most people, like with the Skill Development Zone, rarely experience their Ideal State [Mental]. It often feels like a random event. Something out of our control. Something that just 'happens.' Similar to the Skill Development Zone, the top guitarists, musicians, and performers in the world aren't more 'talented' than you, or 'luckier;' they simply engage with these zones or states more often, so they progress faster. That's the secret. They focus on what produces results; repeating and refining it.

So if we want to maximize our growth as guitarists, we need to access our most resourceful state to practice, perform, and create with. There are many different potential steps you can take to create your Ideal State [Mental], but you want to find what allows you to learn your best, practice your best, and play your best - most consistently. Here are some ideas for accessing your Ideal State [Mental]:

MEDITATION

Pre-practice relaxation:

- It's often thought that meditation is the practice of not thinking. That's simply not true. It's the practice of being aware. Aware of your thoughts, aware of your breath, aware of your body. In that awareness, you hold focus, usually on your breath, a word/phrase, or a mental image. Through consistent focus and deepening relaxation, your thoughts more easily slow down and begin to pass you by; entering a more controlled and resourceful state.

- Your brain actually enters a different brain wave frequency, depending on your level of relaxation, which can greatly improve your learning, Inspiration, and Creativity.

- This can be further enhanced through combining meditation with different technologies like Hemi-Sync which uses binaural beats to shift your brain wave frequency and synchronizes both hemispheres of your brain - producing incredible results.

Focus:

- Another benefit of meditation for guitarists is around the element of focus. If you're practicing guitar and you're able to focus deeper and minimize distraction, then you allow yourself to truly maximize the output of each session.

I highly recommend some sort of meditation practice, in whatever way makes sense for you. Remember - your brain is a computer, you're able to program it. So you want to program it in a way that serves you, and meditation can be a great tool for that.

AFFIRMATIONS/PRAYER

As discussed throughout this book, Beliefs are key to accomplishing anything in life and with guitar. Belief is created from the stories you tell yourself - your internal representations of events, people, situations, and experiences.

I've found that different forms of affirmation and prayer can be highly beneficial for enhancing or shifting Beliefs. They also help remind us of what we want to accomplish [Vision] and the pathway we have laid out towards it [Goals]. They also connect us to a higher potential of ourselves. Our Vision outlines not only *what* we want to accomplish, but also the *person* we want to become.

Think about this - what if you started off each day or practice session with an empowering affirmation like 'I am a Practice Hacker. I Maximize Output While Minimizing Input?' or 'I am a Practice Hacker, I Make the Pinnacle of Others my Foundation?' or 'I'm a Practice Hacker and I don't use excuses, I use what I have?'

You can even do this with your Goals. You can repeat to yourself daily 'I will easily alternate pick [insert piece of music or exercise] at 150bpm using 32nd notes with no mistakes by [insert date].'

Remember: our intentions for the future shape our present moment. By reminding ourselves daily of this higher ideal, it will help us stay on track. It will help calibrate daily action. It will keep us excited, it will keep us driven - especially if we associate positive emotions with them, such as confidence, happiness, fulfilment, warmth, strength, and purpose. So remind yourself daily of your intentions for your future, through affirmations or prayer, and calibrate action accordingly.

Just like our dreams or Vision, we usually have vague ideas of *who* we want to be. We don't often reflect on this, therefore we can't become it. Sometimes, these ideas pop up in our heads, but we generally brush them off. It's something we'll 'get to later' or we tell ourselves 'I'll never be like that, that's just not who I am.'

Is that really any way to live? Your potential just floating around in your head – sometimes peeking out to remind you of your path in life, often in conflict with where you're currently at? Many people experience this, and it often causes them to retreat and create further separation from their path. Sometimes even causing them to seek distraction in destructive behaviours like abusing drugs and alcohol.

Remember: the unknown is uncomfortable, the known is comfortable. To accomplish our Vision and our Goals, we need to go into the unknown. We need to become the person who is capable of creating the results we desire; we need to become more.

Remind yourself daily of the person you want to be, so you can create them.

Keep in mind, affirmations and prayer won't magically create the results you want in life by themselves. Really, they just help focus your mind on who you want to become, or the result you want to create. This allows you to make better decisions in the moment that align with that outcome. However, none of this matters unless you TAKE ACTION.

Dreams are Goals without action. Don't let your dreams remain your dreams. Use affirmations and prayer to help remind you of your path and what you want in life. Get excited. Feel what it's like to accomplish what you desire. Immerse yourself in that experience. Then, each day, do what you can to move towards it. Know that you'll fail - embrace it. Fail more. Fail better.

Stay focused. Stay driven. Remind yourself daily of your path. And most importantly - take action now!

INSPIRATION

Inspiration is an interesting phenomenon. If you imagine Creativity as being a current of new ideas and unrealized potential, Inspiration is like the switch or the trigger that opens up the floodgates. Or, if you imagine Creativity as the internet, Inspiration is like the on/off switch on the modem.

On some level or another, we all have those moments where we feel like our ideas connect and we see the bigger picture. We get goosebumps. We gain clarity. We become excited, we become motivated, and we become driven. We gain new ideas, new insights, and new understandings. We're transported to a new world. It's a powerful feeling.

In my opinion, a key part of being a great musician is understanding how to access and use states of Inspiration as often as possible. Inspiration can act as a source for your Creativity, but can also be used to trigger your Ideal State [Mental]. It can take on many forms, but consider the following:

Movies or videos:

- Maybe a certain scene. The colours, the music, the emotion. It could be a speech. It could even just be a 1-minute clip of the ocean that makes you feel inspired.

- Just pay attention as you're watching movies and videos of what inspires you. Come back to them as needed to recreate that state.

Music [even outside of the genre you're practicing, learning, or writing in]:

- This is hard for a lot of musicians in certain genres, especially within Metal.

- I can tell you from personal experience, that opening up my mind to other genres like Electronic Music, Ambient/New-Age, Pop, and Hip-Hop [among others] has provided me an almost endless source of new Inspiration. Both in terms of accessing and using Creativity, as well as tuning me to my Ideal State [Mental].

- Open your mind, you'll be surprised by what you find.

Books [or audiobooks/podcasts]:

- If you're educating yourself, you're developing your mind. This naturally increases your 'default' which opens you up to new ideas and connections.

- Also, there's often information that just strikes you as profound or shifts the way you think. Whatever it is, capitalize on that state. See how you can repeat that feeling to your benefit.

- Learning and growing in any area can help with creative endeavours as well as raise all Foundations of your life to a higher level. Keep your brain learning, keep your brain moving, and discover what inspires you.

Being in nature:

- Nature can really help cultivate Inspiration. Not everyone appreciates nature the same, but there's something so connected and organic about being immersed in it - at least for me. It makes me feel more alive. I find the fresh air and sunlight to be rejuvenating. For others, this might be the rain or the moonlight.

- Being in nature removes us from a lot of the EMF radiation that we're all exposed to. For me, it helps minimize distraction, allowing me to think more deeply. I'm able to receive and understand the answers to my problems with greater clarity and ease, as well as access deeper levels of Inspiration and Creativity.

Comedy:

- Laughter is such a beautiful aspect of being human. It can help trigger states of Inspiration through joy, elation, and other powerful emotions.

- Consider compiling a list of jokes, videos, or other material that can easily provoke laughter and cultivate a state of Inspiration.

Negative States:

- There's something to be said about using negative states for Inspiration. Whether anger, sadness, despair, confusion, or hopelessness - as creative individuals we seek to express emotion. We'll often create something to tell a story about what we're experiencing. Or, if we're lacking a certain emotion, we'll create something to try and fill that hole.

- A lot of artists go even further by exploring destructive states, like those found through abusing drugs or alcohol. However, I don't recommend this. It's dangerous, unsustainable, and your art, life, and those around you will suffer as a result.

Spirituality/Religion:

- Many people's Inspiration comes from their spiritual or religious practice. By opening up to greater potentials of life and being, this may influence and inspire new ideas. Some of the greatest works in art, music, and writing throughout history were inspired by spirituality/religion.

Other People:

- Other people can be your greatest source Inspiration, however, you might not always have other people around so you shouldn't rely on them solely.
- Whether it's family, friends, or working with other creative individuals - the combination of multiple people influencing each other or working together can often be the perfect formula for accessing Inspiration as well as discovering new sources of Creativity.

I highly suggest taking the healthier, more controlled approaches to Inspiration. However, if you experience a negative state, absolutely use it to transmute your suffering into something that can benefit you as well as those around you. The creation of music is cathartic. Use it in the ways you need to.

You can use any of these sources of Inspiration to put you into your Ideal State [Mental], as well as directly influence your Creativity. Find what works best for you. Control your state. Control your outcome.

EXERCISE

We will discuss exercise more in **Secret 18**, but it allows us to get our blood flowing and our heart rate up, which means not only does this wake-up our body, but also our mind. We're more easily able to access energy, mental clarity, focus, Inspiration, and therefore Creativity. It also improves our ability to learn.

ROUTINE/RITUAL

As you know, to establish a new Habit, it's important to include it in some sort of daily [ideally morning] routine. This is also called a ritual. It's just a matter of repeating something for a desired effect. This might be as simple as having a cup of coffee before each practice session. Maybe it's a certain snack or a drink. Maybe it's a certain sequence of events or actions. It could be one of the Inspiration factors previously listed, or any other combination of things unique to you.

These become ways to produce your Ideal State [Mental] and they are incredibly valuable. They should be something you seek to actively engage with and control. Once you've discovered the best triggers to immerse yourself within your Ideal State [Mental], you want to repeat this sequence before every practice.

Through perfected repetition of your routine or ritual, you'll be strengthening and enhancing its connection to your Ideal State [Mental]. This means that you'll be able to access it faster, and explore with far greater depth. As a result, you'll continually increase the benefits of each practice session - allowing you to more easily gain Achievement Momentum. This will encourage you to stick with your practice, which will allow you to quickly form a new Habit. You can take this a step further by doing something called Anchoring.

ANCHORING

Anchoring is a Neurolinguistic Programming [NLP] technique, which has been popularized by people like Tony Robbins. However, it's a natural part of our neurological processes - we just haven't always been in control of it. That is, until now.

If you look at many top individuals, you'll notice that they have some sort of routine or ritual they perform before they go on stage, play their big game, give a speech, etc. Routines and rituals are key to controlling your state. They have limitations however, because you can't always control your circumstances. If you rely on using a particular routine or ritual to enter your Ideal State [Mental], then what happens if you don't have time for it? What happens if your environment changes, or the situation around you is out of your control?

This is where Anchoring comes into play.

Anchoring is really as simple as linking a unique movement or action to your Ideal State [Mental]. You can also link it to any other mental state, memory, or emotion that you wish to access at will. Through perfected repetition of this unique movement or action, you're Encoding the association between it and the state that you're in. Then, when you're outside of that state, you simply need to reproduce that unique movement or action and you'll put yourself back into the desired state.

The Anchor might be as simple as clenching your fist a certain way, or spinning around and clapping in a particular fashion. It might be a specific finger and hand action combined with a phrase. It can be anything, but it has to be something unique to the state you want to Anchor. Just using a common movement or phrase might not be enough, as those connections are already deeply Encoded.

However, creating a brand new Anchor, and enforcing it with high energy and high emotion at the peak of your Ideal State [Mental], will allow you to easily and strongly form that new connection. It will associate it *only* with that state. No rewiring of previous connections needed. Which means it can be easily accessed at will. To properly Encode this, repeat this Anchoring process 3-7 times in a row, or as needed, using perfected repetition. It has to be *exactly* the same each time, otherwise it won't work. Then, whenever you need to access your Ideal State [Mental], use your Anchor.

For more information on this concept, I highly recommend reading *Unlimited Power* by Tony Robbins. Additionally, you can find a lot of information regarding NLP online.

Anchoring is truly an elite-level method for controlling your state. This is one of the most important tools used by some the greatest individuals in the world, yet is virtually unknown to the average person. Use it to your advantage and accelerate your progress beyond what you ever dreamed possible - in guitar, and life.

#2 IDEAL STATE [PHYSICAL]

Most people will use scales, chromatic runs, and different exercises to warm-up. These are better than nothing, but they aren't really beneficial to your practice session. Think of it like this: if you're going for a run, do you warm-up with bicep curls? If you're going to play hockey, do you warm-up in a football field? I'd imagine the answer is no.

As Practice Hackers, we're looking to be maximally effective with our practice. This means our warm-ups need to reflect that. Why waste time and effort doing something unnecessary?

Our warm-ups should be mini practice sessions in themselves, further strengthening the Foundations on which our practice is built. Depending on what your practice session requires from you, you should formulate a warm-up based on that. I have divided this into two main phases:

PHASE I: WARM UP

1. Get your blood flowing.

    • Jogging, push-ups, jumping jacks, etc.

2. Massage your arms, fingers, and shoulders.

- Think of all of the parts of your body you will be using. Massage all of them. Go along the muscle fibers. Loosen everything up, especially if you're cold.

3. Stretch your arms, fingers, and shoulders.

- There are a few different options here, but think about the movements your fingers and hands make and stretch back and forth along those pathways. Perform arm and hand circles. Just make sure everything is stretched out and ready to go.

PHASE II: SPEED UP

1. Whatever you're working on, begin at what your *current* Baseline is. This is done by finding the 'comfortable' pace in which you're able to play the part correctly.

2. Start with a metronome, and ensure you're playing the part perfectly. Encode it 3-7 times in a row, through perfected repetition, without a single mistake. Then increase the BPM by 5-10 [I prefer 7]. Every time you increase the BPM, ensure you're Encoding it 3-7 times and repeat this until you're at your working speed,

3. To ensure you're playing it perfectly, refer to the Performance Measurements in **Secret 7**. The main ones to pay attention to are: Efficiency of Motion, Fluidity of Motion, Pitch, Rhythm, and Timing.

The goal with all of this is to find the minimal amount of warming up to create the optimal starting point for practice - our Ideal State [Physical].

Note: You might be learning something brand new and not have enough of it memorized or worked out to warm-up with as suggested above. In this case, I recommend finding something similar to what you're working on, using a similar technique or set of movements, and build it up in the same way. We're just looking to warm-up based on the task at hand, versus random exercises that don't connect to what we're working on. Don't overthink it.

#3 MENTAL + AURAL PRACTICE

Use Mental and Aural practice in preparation for your Physical practice session. This can help you pre-learn or familiarize yourself with the material before actually working on it - making Physical practice much easier. This is similar to viewing a map of somewhere that you want to travel to before embarking on the journey. If you become familiar with the outline of the area, and the terrain, it enhances the depth in which you can explore it.

With guitar practice, this primes your brain for the session. It's like knowing the questions for the test so as you study, your brain automatically seeks out the answers. You're pre-establishing your Foundation. This makes building into Pinnacles and creating new Foundations much easier, and quicker.

Prior to Physical practice, ensure that you're listening to the piece multiple times [Aural practice]. This can be done directly before Physical practice, or even earlier in the day. Also, try to visualize where the parts are on the fretboard [Mental practice]. Imagine yourself playing it. Really feel it and experience it. You'll know you have this down when you're able to hear the piece and/or visualize yourself playing it without needing to listen to it.

Repeated use of Mental and Aural practice helps you pre-establish new connections *prior* to Physical practice as well as strengthen them *after* Physical practice. As you can see, this compounds the effects of each Physical practice session; greatly increasing the results you will get.

Early on, when practicing or learning a piece, you'll want to include *both* Mental and Aural practice. But once you've established strong enough connections, you'll want to focus primarily on Mental practice, as it will recall directly from your memory; strengthening the connections you've made.

IDEAL STATE AND THE REAL WORLD

These are some different examples of Ideal State in action:

- Before every match in which Johnny Kerr was commentating, Michael Jordan would take Talcum Powder, go up to Johnny Kerr, and do a powder clap.
- The New Zealand All Blacks do the Haka [a Maori War Dance] prior to every Rugby match.
- John Legend is known for eating a rotisserie chicken before going on stage.
- Keith Richards requires a shepherd's pie before he'll perform, and has to break the crust himself. In fact, at one show in Toronto, the security staff ate his shepherd's pie and the show was delayed until a new one was made.
- Tony Robbins has an intense pre-show ritual, but one of the Anchors he uses right before he jumps on stage is an air-punch and spin move.

When you're at the top of your game, or desire to get there, there's very little room for error. You can't waste time. You can't waste energy. You need to operate at your best, as often as you can. This is what differentiates the elite from the average. Most people don't know how to access their Ideal State, and their entire life suffers because of it. However, those who do know how to access it are able to skyrocket to heights untold. Is it because they are lucky? Is it because they are more talented? Is it because they are better than you? No. They simply understand how to access their Ideal State at will - which is a key part of the framework that produces the results they have.

HOW TO APPLY THIS

To create your Ideal State [Synergy], you must engage both your Ideal State [Mental] and Ideal State [Physical].

There are many ways to access your Ideal State [Mental], but find whatever puts you into your most resourceful and productive state. Once you're there, create an Anchor and Encode it through perfected repetition so you can easily access it at will. This is critical to elite performance.

Then, you want to access your Ideal State [Physical] by getting your blood moving, massaging and stretching the muscles you'll be using, and then building up to working speed with the piece you'll be practicing.

> **Practice Hacker Tip:** Use Anchors to control your state, control your life, and gain the edge.

Secret 17

The Elite Framework

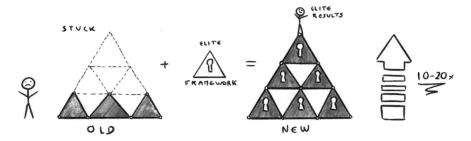

The Old Framework is outdated and limiting. It creates subpar results. The Elite Framework is the key to becoming the guitarist you've always dreamed of being without needing to practice all day. It creates Elite Results. This is the secret formula.

Here we are. Everything in this book has built up to this very moment. The Elite Framework.

We're always told the same thing when it comes to improving on guitar: *practice more.* Do you want to be a great guitarist? *Practice more.* Do you want to improve your speed, your songwriting, and even your learning abilities? *Practice more.* They always say you just need to put *more* time in, yet there's no real discussion on *how* that time is spent. It's always about practicing exercises, learning new songs, or learning different Techniques or Theory.

But how do you address mistakes? Do you just repeat the entire piece over and over again? Or do you focus on specific areas? Which areas do you focus on first? How do you actually fix them? How do you increase the speed? What happens when you hit a Limit? How do you reintegrate parts you've fixed into the whole piece? Is there an order or sequence to do all of this?

You'd think, with a practice framework, all of these questions would be answered. However, with the Old Framework, they aren't. Perhaps a teacher or resource can give you different ideas or tips to patch up issues as they arise. However, I look at this like a doctor prescribing medication for a *symptom*, without addressing the *root cause* of the issue.

The main difference between the Old Framework and The Elite Framework, is that The Elite Framework is built around addressing the root cause of the issue; *how* you are learning and practicing. It focuses *only* on what's responsible for growth: the Skill Development Zone. The Old Framework is lucky if it ever touches this zone in a session - nevermind for more than a few minutes. As a result, so much talent and potential is wasted - making the world a darker place.

THE OLD FRAMEWORK

- To be great, you need to put in more time, you need to practice more [while the rest of your life suffers as a result].

- Focuses on the 'what' of learning, not the 'how' [gives the illusion of progress while actually holding you back].

- Progress happens slowly, even with lessons [wasting thousands of dollars, and hundreds of hours a year ineffectively practicing].

- Doesn't address the root cause of your limitations [wasting your time, building destructive habits, and creating vast imbalances in your playing].

- Only engages the Skill Development Zone, which is solely responsible for progress, for 3-6 minutes per 60-minute practice session on average [the rest is wasted time, energy, and money].

- Holds you back from your potential [making it impossible to become the guitarist you've always dreamed of being and impacting the world with your music].

This is because the Old Framework's practice session often looks like this:

- Sit down and pick up the guitar
- Run a few exercises
- Try playing some different riffs you like
- Start jamming or improvising something
- Try learning a new song, riff, solo, or bit of Theory
- Try working on a new Technique
- Maybe you even try writing something

Then, it's done and you're no further ahead than you were before. You're switching between all of these unrelated exercises and skills, never sticking with them long enough to actually engage the Skill Development Zone [the precise point in which skill growth occurs]. Even worse - you're not actually practicing what is most likely to help you achieve your Goals or Vision. In fact, if you're following the Old Framework, you likely don't even have clear Goals or a clear Vision...

Think of all of the guitarists you know who have been playing for 20, 30, 50+ years and haven't gotten any better than when they first started. It's obviously not just a matter of having 'more time.' It's not just a matter of practicing the perfect Technique, piece of Theory, or any of the other million things you can learn on guitar.

My issue was that I was always focused on 'what' I was practicing. I thought maybe I'd figure out the right trick or pattern that would unlock everything. Was I ever wrong. Again, it's like a doctor prescribing medication to deal with the symptom, without addressing the root cause of the issue. As a result, nothing changes and over time your issues only become worse - even fatal.

In my search for answers, it became clear that *what* I was practicing wasn't the issue. Yes, it does matter, but mostly in the broader context of your Goals and what you're trying to achieve as a guitarist; your Vision.

I realized I needed to change **how** I was practicing. Without the right approach to learning and practice, it doesn't matter what your Goals are - you'll be lucky to make *any* progress at all. Without the right system, progress will happen very slowly, and over a long period of time. You'll put in hours and hours of work, sacrificing other areas of your life, and for what?

Any small amount of progress you make only reinforces the false idea that to get better you need to dedicate more time. Also, because the majority of your practice isn't focused around the Skill Development Zone, you're spending most of your session reinforcing destructive and limiting practice habits. This means whatever progress you *are* making will come to a screeching halt. And quickly.

Your Foundation is everything. If your Foundation is weak, you cannot build to great heights. If your Foundation is weak, everything will collapse.

This isn't sustainable. This isn't how elite musicians practice. As Practice Hackers, this isn't how we practice anymore. It's no wonder so many guitarists give up or fail to reach their potential. It's because of the Old Framework. And I'm here to help change that.

To shift how we approach practice, we need to shift our frameworks. The Old Framework produces predictable and subpar results. Practice like a Beginner. Play like a Beginner.

If the Old Framework was truly the best way to practice, wouldn't everyone be an elite guitarist? Guitar practice isn't just some magical skill that some people are good at and others aren't. There are real mechanisms at play that are responsible for growth. Understanding them and engaging with them unlocks progress on guitar. It's as simple as that. How far you're able to push that is up to you, and you alone.

The difference between the world's greatest guitarists and you, is that *you* have been using the Old Framework. Most people do. In fact, I did most of my life. It's really all we're taught. However, the greatest musicians in the world - elite musicians, use a different framework. They use The Elite Framework.

THE ELITE FRAMEWORK

- To be great, you need to optimize every second of your session. Practice less to grow more [allowing all areas of your life to improve as a result].

- Focuses on the 'how' of learning, not so much the 'what' [allows you to easily progress and move forward quickly].

- Progress happens exponentially, especially with lessons [saving thousands of dollars, and hundreds of hours a year by effectively practicing].

- Your entire session is built around addressing and fixing the root cause of your limitations [saving you time, building constructive habits, and achieving balance, precision, and control over your playing].

- Engages the Skill Development Zone, which is solely responsible for progress, for your entire session [increasing the results of each practice by 10-20x minimum - saving time, energy, and money].

- Allows you to not only uncover your potential, but to become it - becoming more [making it possible to become the guitarist you've always dreamed of being, impacting the world with your music].

The elite's practice session often looks like this:

- Sit down in your Space of Productivity which is *designed* for practice.

- Prepare for practice by accessing your Ideal State [Mental] along with your Ideal State [Physical] - creating Ideal State [Synergy].

- Prime your mind for the session with Mental/Aural practice.

- Work on your Goals in Practice Sprints, taking Effective Breaks in-between.
- Use The Elite Framework to constantly push the Skill Development Zone for your entire Sprint.
- Track your progress daily, weekly, and monthly to analyze and optimize your progress - using Biohacks and Practice Variables to blast through plateaus [as we will discuss in **Secret 18**].

As you can tell, there is only *one* system that's designed to produce elite results, and it isn't the Old Framework. Because I didn't have this system, I nearly gave up on guitar. I nearly gave up on the one thing that provided me the greatest joy, purpose, and fulfilment in my life: music. I was at my lowest point, yet there were people around me who were passing me by, and quickly. How was I going to catch up? What were they doing that I wasn't? It's simple. Whether aware of it or not, they were engaging with The Elite Framework, at least on some level. Those with greater results? They were engaging with it even more.

It's incredible really. As you go through The Elite Framework, you'll be blown away by the hundreds, if not thousands of hours you've likely been practicing guitar ineffectively. Not to mention the thousands of dollars you've likely wasted on lessons and other resources - without having the proper system to optimize *how* you're learning and practicing.

When I had this realization, as empowering as it was… it was also very difficult to come to terms with. For so long I had wasted my time, energy, and money. I was even on the brink of giving up. If I had this system years ago, who knows where I would be right now.

But ultimately, this led me on an incredible journey to discover what set the greatest guitarists, musicians, and performers apart from the rest. How did they practice? It took me years of research, testing, and analysis - but through all of that work, I discovered and synthesized the Practice Secrets of the Pros, and more importantly: The Elite Framework. Now, it is yours. All of the secrets are yours.

I believe you have the power to change the world with your music. Whether it's just to improve for yourself, to share music with friends and family, to teach music, or to be the next great virtuoso - you should be able to pursue your dream to its fullest, without needing to sacrifice every waking moment to practice. The last thing this world needs is another person with so much potential giving up because the road is too difficult due to using the Old Framework. The world needs your music. The world needs *you*.

The fact that you own this book right now is a game changer and I truly mean that. You have an advantage unlike any other time in history. In the past, such information was only available to the few who were able to figure it out on their own, or received the right mentorship. But now you have *the* system responsible for turning average guitarists into the guitarists they've always dreamed of being without needing to practice all day. The system to transform you from zero to hero in record time. You have the Practice Secrets of the Pros.

Most importantly, you have The Elite Framework. Make this your Foundation and watch your potential unfold. Create the results you've always desired with complete ease, freedom, speed, and confidence. Your future is in your hands. Become your potential. Become more.

PRISM OF ANALYSIS

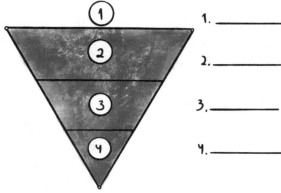

1. _____

2. _____

3. _____

4. _____

The Prism of Analysis houses the 4 Focus Levels, also known as Levels of Resolution.

The Prism of Analysis is a visual representation of the Focus Levels, moving from the *largest* Level of Resolution to the *smallest*.

FOCUS LEVELS

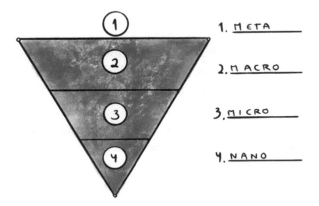

1. META
2. MACRO
3. MICRO
4. NANO

The 4 Focus Levels: [1] Meta [song/piece], [2] Macro [section], [3] Micro [measure], [4] Nano [note].

When learning or practicing a piece of music, you want to approach it at multiple Levels of Resolution [i.e Focus Levels].

1. META [SONG/PIECE] LEVEL - START HERE

- This is where you develop the outline. As we learned in **Secret 7**, Mental/Aural practice is the best way to prepare yourself for what you'll be working on. You'll know you have this down once you're able to play back the part in your head and/or visualize it without needing to listen to it.

- Additionally, you can approach the piece without any previous knowledge, and try to get through it a few times at full speed, mistakes and all. Though you won't be playing it correctly, you get to experience your Limits while also priming your mind and body for the task at hand. This allows you to go deeper during your practice, and make progress quicker.

- Both methods establish a map or outline of the structure, the emotion, the melodies, the rhythms, and the transitions among other things.

- Once you've done this, shift focus to the Macro [section] level.

2. MACRO [SECTION] LEVEL

- This usually refers to a larger part of the song/piece such as the verse, chorus, solo, or bridge.

- Start with the *hardest* section first and begin working through it [the exact process to do this is described in the Pathway to Completion sequence in the next section of this book].

- By working on the hardest part first, you're focusing on what will require most of your energy. By accomplishing that, the rest of the song/piece will be much easier to learn and work on.

- Remember, we're looking to address Weak Points and improve them. The hardest part = your Weakest Point. This is true on every Focus Level.

- The problem is that most people will repeat an *entire section* over and over again, hoping to eventually correct where the mistake is happening [Weak Point]. This appears to make sense on the surface, but is actually very detrimental. If your problem is within a specific measure, or even a group of notes, by practicing the *whole* section to fix it, you're never addressing your Weak Points directly. This means it takes longer to fix the problem, and it also brings up *both* your Weak Points and your strong points - creating more imbalances and actually wasting your practice sessions.

- When you run into issues and mistakes at the Macro [section] level, address them at the Micro [measure] level.

3. MICRO [MEASURE] LEVEL

- Even within a section, it's not likely that the *entire* section is causing you problems. Issues usually occur when a pattern changes, the tempo changes, the rhythm/pulse/time-signature changes, or a transition takes place.
- Begin working through this level, learning, and building up the part properly [as described in the Pathway to Completion sequence].
- When you run into issues and mistakes at the Micro [measure] level, address them at the Nano [note] level.

4. NANO [NOTE] LEVEL

- The final Level of Resolution is the note level.
- Even within a measure, it's not likely that the *entire* measure is causing you problems. Issues usually occur when a pattern changes, the tempo changes, the rhythm/pulse/time-signature changes, or a transition takes place.
- Instead of repeating the entire measure, address the issue *precisely* where it happens. Go note-by-note if needed, and follow the Pathway to Completion sequence to fix and build it back up.

Now that we understand that there are multiple levels to practice, we should begin at the largest Level of Resolution and focus on the most difficult parts first. When an issue arises, we need to Focus Shift to a smaller Level of Resolution and work through the problem. Then, once the problem is fixed and built back up to the previous level, we need to reintegrate it with surrounding material at that level. This happens at each level: Nano, Micro, Macro, and Meta.

PATHWAY TO COMPLETION SEQUENCE OUTLINE

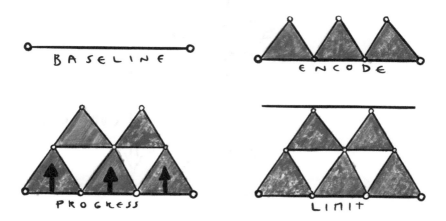

The Baseline is established. The Encoding process integrates/automates the information [strengthening the Foundation]. As a result, higher Foundations are established and Progress begins [building]. This continues until a Limit is reached [Encoding at each new level].

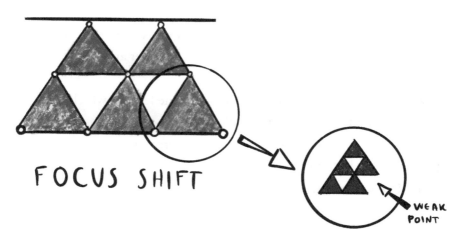

When the limit is reached we must Focus Shift to a smaller Level of Resolution to address the specific issue [Weak Point] where it occurs at the appropriate level [Macro, Micro, or Nano]. Then we fix and re-integrate it using the Pathway to Completion sequence.

PATHWAY TO COMPLETION SEQUENCE

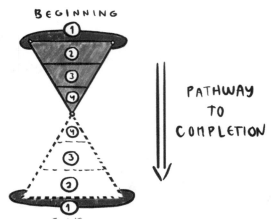

[1] Meta, [2] Macro, [3] Micro, [4] Nano The Pathway to Completion starts from the highest level of resolution [Meta] and zooms into the lowest level of resolution [Nano]. Weak Points are addressed then reintegrated at each level of resolution, until completion [Meta].

BASELINE

- This is the *comfortable* speed in which you're able to *correctly* perform the part you're working on, whether at the Meta, Macro, Micro, or Nano level.

- This should be the tempo *just* below the level in which you begin making mistakes [your Limit].

- Focus on your Performance Measurements to ensure you're playing it *perfectly* at this speed.

- **Use a metronome.**

ENCODE

- Once you've established your Baseline, you want to Encode the *correct* patterns through *perfected repetition*. Do this by repeating the part 3-7 times in a row without a single mistake, focusing on your Performance Measurements. The more repetitions, the stronger the connections, which means the deeper you'll integrate and automate the part.

- If you mess up once, start again until you can repeat the part 3-7 times in a row, *perfectly*.
- This is how you establish your Foundation to begin building. This is critical.
- **Use a metronome.**

PROGRESS

- After you've Encoded correctly at your Baseline, you want to incrementally increase the tempo by 5-10 BPM [I recommend starting with 7]. You can also do less, if needed.
- At each new tempo, you need to Encode with *perfected repetition*, focusing on your Performance Measurements. This establishes higher Foundations, making it easier to build to your target speed.
- **Use a metronome.**

LIMIT

- You'll repeat the Progress step, pushing yourself and getting uncomfortable, until you hit your Limit [where a few mistakes begin to happen].
- Identify and focus on one issue at a time. This will likely be the Weak Point that you previously outlined when you were setting your Goals.
- Ideally, you will just increase the tempo and Encode until you hit your target speed, however, you will likely begin making mistakes before you get there - this is your Limit.
- **Use a metronome.**

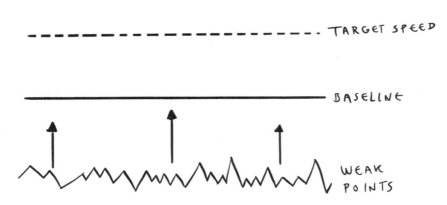

Here we can see that our Baseline is actually below our target speed, and there are Weak Points that we need to address. Our focus is simply to bring everything up to our Baseline, focusing on the most difficult parts first [Weak Points], and then build our Baseline towards our target speed.

FOCUS SHIFT

- To fix an issue, go down a Focus Level in the Prism of Analysis.
- For example, if you're at the Macro Level, go down to the Micro Level.
- Repeat the previous steps for this new level. This means establishing a new Baseline, correctly Encoding the part, and then building it back up through the Progress step until you reach the Baseline that you previously established.
- If you end up hitting a Limit, you simply go down another Focus Level and repeat these steps.
- The goal is to identify the problem *precisely* where it happens, zoom in, fix it, build it back up, and then reintegrate it.

LIMIT BREAKER: Though the Pathway to Completion sequence has a built-in system for identifying, repairing, and pushing beyond Limits, if you continue getting stuck, one of the best ways to blast through it is by using a Limit Breaker. A Limit Breaker is a type of Practice Variable [as we will discuss in **Secret 18**].

There are two types of Limit Breakers:

- Limit Breaker [Lite]: Practice at 10-15bpm above your Baseline or target speed

- Limit Breaker [Insanity]: Practice at double your Baseline or target speed

Whatever you choose, get uncomfortable and push yourself for as long as you can during your Practice Sprint. You'll make a *lot* of mistakes, but the focus here is to stimulate your mind and body with this new adaptation requirement [Limit Breaker]. You're priming your circuits. Then, when you bring it back down to your previous Baseline or even your target speed, it's going to feel a *lot* easier to play. Use this as much as needed during your practice session.

REINTEGRATION

- The final piece of the Pathway to Completion sequence.

- Once you've fixed your Weak Point, Encoded it, and built it up to your previous Baseline - you need to reintegrate it with the surrounding material of the previous level.

- To reintegrate it, you simply Encode it.

- Levels of Reintegration

  - If working at the Nano [note] level, reintegrate with surrounding notes within the measure.

  - If working at the Micro [measure] level, reintegrate with surrounding measures or the entire Macro [section] level.

  - If working at the Macro [section] level, reintegrate with surrounding sections or additional measures.

- Repeat this as needed, starting from the most difficult parts to the easiest, until you can finally reintegrate all parts of the whole; the Meta [song/piece] level.

Once you've properly repaired, built up, and reintegrated all parts with the whole, you want to use the Pathway to Completion sequence again to bring everything up to your target speed - if you aren't already there.

This is why The Elite Framework is so powerful - more specifically, the Pathway to Completion sequence. You're properly identifying the root cause of your Limits, fixing them quickly, and building them back up to where you need them. As a result, you're able to spend your entire session at the edge of your capabilities, pushing the Skill Development Zone, which we know is solely responsible for progress. As you go through this process, you're *only* focusing on what your Weak Points are. You're not wasting your time or energy.

This method truly maximizes what you get out of each session. In fact, using this method will allow you to make more progress in a month than many make in a year or more - I'm not exaggerating. If progress happens by pushing the Skill Development Zone, then what's going to create more progress? Spending 3-6 minutes in that zone per 60-minute session, or 60? You do the math.

PATHWAY TO COMPLETION SEQUENCE EXAMPLE:

Say you're working on the **verse** of a song [Macro level] at 120bpm, but a specific **measure** [Micro level] is causing you trouble. Instead of repeating the *entire* **verse** over and over again, you'll just focus on fixing the **measure**. First, you'll establish a new Baseline for the **measure** [say 100bpm] and then you'll Encode it through perfected repetition and build the **measure** up until it's at 120bpm [your previous Baseline].

However, say you're hitting a Limit with the **measure** before you get to your target speed of 120bpm, then you want to identify the particular **group of notes** [Nano level] where the issue is occurring. This usually happens when a pattern changes, the tempo changes, the rhythm/pulse/ time-signature changes, or a transition takes place. You'll then establish a new Baseline for that **group of notes** [say it's 90bpm]. After that, you'll properly Encode those **notes**, and then build up to the Baseline of the previous part [in this case, the **measure**, which we established as 100bpm].

Once it's brought up to the Baseline of the previous part, you want to reintegrate it with the surrounding material. So if you are working on a **group of notes** and you build it up to the Baseline of the **measure**, you'll want to reintegrate that **group of notes** with the rest of the **measure**.

Because you've already built it up to speed, you should be able to run through the whole **measure** now. If not, identify exactly where the issue happens, Focus Shift, and run through the Pathway to Completion sequence to repair it.

Then, once the entire **measure** is repaired, you will Encode it and build it up to the Baseline of the **verse** you originally established [120bpm]. Once there, you will reintegrate the **measure** with the **verse**. Again, because you've already built it up to speed, you should be able to run through the whole **verse** now. If not, identify exactly where the issue happens, Focus Shift, and run through the Pathway to Completion sequence to repair it.

Usually when you reintroduce a fixed part back to where it came from, the issues that arise are around the transitions before and after the part you just fixed. If that's the case, simply identify exactly where the issue happens, Focus Shift, and run through the Pathway to Completion sequence to repair it.

Repeat this until you've addressed every issue, at every level. You want to start first with the most difficult parts of what you're working on, and fix issues where they occur. Then, once the entire **song** is at a consistent Baseline, and all of the Weak Points have been fixed, you can then build it up to your target speed by repeating the Pathway to Completion sequence.

See how this process works? You're simply focusing on the most difficult part first [your Weakest Point]. You're establishing a Baseline - where you can play the part comfortably and correctly. Then, as you're Encoding and building it up, you're recognizing mistakes as you approach your Limit. You take one issue at a time, Focus Shift, establish a new Baseline, properly Encode it, and build it back up to the Baseline of previous level. Then, you reintegrate it with that previous level, and repeat this process as needed.

You're only fixing what you need to fix, and quickly. This is the secret. This is The Elite Framework.

PATHWAY TO COMPLETION SEQUENCE SUMMARY

It's easy to get lost in the details, but I want to further simplify this process for you:

- Use a Metronome.
- **Baseline**: establish the speed in which you can comfortably perform the part correctly.
- **Encode:** properly integrate and automate the part through perfected repetition.
- **Progress:** incrementally increase the tempo while Encoding at each new level.
- **Limit:** stop when you begin making a few small mistakes.
- **Focus Shift:** focus on one mistake at a time. Repeat the previous steps at a smaller Level of Resolution.
- If you struggle getting past your Limit, use a **Limit Breaker**.
- **Repeat** this sequence as needed until...
- **Reintegration:** once the issue is correct and built up to the previous Baseline, reintegrate it with surrounding material at that level.

- Once all parts of the whole are fixed and at your original Baseline, build *everything* up to your target speed [if you aren't already there], using the previous steps.

One thing to note is that the learning process isn't linear. You might find that when an issue comes up on the Macro level, you address it at the Nano Level, and then reintegrate it at the Meta level. You might also find that you can increase the tempo more than 5-10BPM during the Progress step.

Address problems on the level you need to, in the ways that serve you best. Use this sequence as a guide or template and make it your Foundation, but ultimately find what works best for you.

SKILL DEVELOPMENT ZONE

Throughout this book, I have mentioned the Skill Development Zone quite frequently. It's the key area in which progress takes place. But what is it exactly?

Simply put, the Skill Development Zone is our point of adaptation.

When it comes to lifting weights, we know that growth happens in the last few reps. A good program understands this, identifies Limits, and systematically pushes them in the ways required for growth. If you work out too much, you risk overtraining. Too little, you won't grow. If your workouts are too random, there are too many variables and you don't know what's working and what's not. If they are too repetitive, your body will quickly adapt; stopping progress.

The same principles apply to music practice.

See, anyone can go into the gym and do random exercises and see *some* results - but that's <u>only</u> in the beginning. Once the 'beginner gains' wear off, so does any progress and momentum they once had.

This, unfortunately, is what happens to many guitarists who follow the Old Framework. They make progress initially, because there is a lot of new stimulation - their mind and body are trying to adapt. They'll put in hours and hours of practice, not even aware that they are reinforcing destructive and limiting habits. Then, once their 'beginner gains' wear off, they are stuck. The Foundation they built can't support further growth. They can't recognize or engage their Limits. They can't make progress.

This is where many people give up. They just assume they're as good as they'll ever get. Maybe they just aren't talented enough or weren't born 'naturally gifted' like others. Maybe guitar just isn't for them. Maybe if they had *all day* to practice, *then* they'd be able to make progress like they used to - life's just too busy now. Sound familiar?

These are all **excuses**. They are comforting lies, but lies nonetheless. They are Limiting Beliefs. They protect our ego. They justify our shortcomings and they alleviate us from taking responsibility for our actions. They are convenient, but serve no one.

To make progress, real progress, we need a protocol that's designed around engaging the Skill Development Zone. One that organizes practice in a way that focuses primarily on identifying Weak Points [Limits], repairing them, building them back up, reintegrating them, and pushing beyond previous adaptation. A system that controls for variables so we can understand what's working and what isn't - making adjustments as needed to continue growth.

This is why we need to use The Elite Framework, and more specifically the Pathway to Completion sequence. Without it, we're only hoping to make progress, but we don't actually know if we're pushing our Limits correctly, or at all. If we don't push our Limits, we won't grow. It's as simple as that.

The quicker you can identify your Limits, the quicker you can fix them, which means the quicker you can push beyond previous adaptation. The more that you properly do this, the more efficient you'll become at engaging the Skill Development Zone. This means that you will continue to optimize every second of your practice over time - exponentially increasing your results with each practice; freeing up your time and energy. Putting you on the path to becoming the guitarist you've always dreamed of being!

But keep in mind, engaging this zone can be very uncomfortable - as it should be. You don't grow in comfort. You need to *really* push yourself mentally and physically during your Practice Sprints. The greater the emotional response, the greater the depth of learning. Push your Limits and get uncomfortable, but be smart - don't risk injury. This is where we grow!

IMPORTANT NOTE

Though the entire practice session, if following the Pathway to Completion sequence, is predicated on breaking Limits, there are still sticking points that can occur. This is where Limit Breakers or other Practice Variables usually come into play [as we will discuss in **Secret 18**]. But even if you're struggling to make progress *during* a particular session, as long as you're constantly pushing your Limits with properly Encoded patterns and movements, you will still grow. You're creating and strengthening connections. By engaging your Limits [point of adaptation], you're encouraging your mind and body to adapt to the stimulation; therefore raising your Foundation.

So don't get discouraged if you struggle to make progress during a session. Whether you see results *during* practice, or *after*, you're still making progress if you're engaging the Skill Development Zone. Push your Limits, increase the need for adaptation, develop higher Foundations, get uncomfortable, and watch your progress skyrocket!

BUT WHAT ABOUT THEORY AND CREATIVITY?

We can see that the Pathway to Completion sequence and the Skill Development Zone apply to building Technique and learning music, but what about Theory and Creativity?

For Theory and Creativity, it's simply a matter of identifying Limits. Then, you just need to engage them in a way that you can control, allowing you to actually measure progress. We can use the Pathway to Completion sequence to do this, but there are other ways as well.

THEORY

You can apply the Pathway to Completion sequence here by learning pieces of music or even exercises that use the Theory you're wanting to learn. This can help you quickly and easily learn it in a musical context, which puts you further along the Knowledge/Integration Framework [as outlined in **Secret 6**]. What's also beneficial about this method, is that if you're learning a piece of music or even an exercise that you enjoy or love, it elicits a higher emotional response which enhances your depth of learning.

However, simply learning Theory in a musical context won't be enough on its own. As discussed in **Secret 6**, we need to *integrate* it and the best way to do that is through the Master Approach: creating with it.

CREATIVITY

With Creativity, we can engage the Pathway to Completion sequence, but this is done a bit differently. In terms of writing, we do this through building the song, riff, or solo in layers; starting from simplicity and evolving and expanding into complexity.

For example, when writing a riff, we need to establish the outline first [let's say this is a chord progression]. By starting here, and Encoding it, we internalize its structure, which means we can focus on exploring it without having to try and memorize the initial outline.

The next step might be to work out a rhythm to help the chord progression flow. After we've developed a basic idea of the rhythm, we Encode it, and continue this process. At each level of Encoding, we're adding something new to evolve the part melodically and rhythmically; adding variance, movement, embellishment, or anything else we desire.

This is especially helpful if we're trying to write with new Techniques or Theory, or if we're writing at a speed or level of technical ability that we currently struggle with. We can use the Pathway to Completion sequence to quickly integrate and build up the new part we've written, which addresses Weak Points, establishes new Foundations, and greatly improves our Productivity as well as Creativity.

The faster we're able to internalize what we're writing as we're writing it, the quicker we can explore new creative ideas, and the greater detail in which we can express them. All of this, without losing sight of the original Inspiration and losing the forest for the trees.

OTHER WAYS TO ENGAGE THE SKILL DEVELOPMENT ZONE

The Skill Development Zone applies to everything - it's simply a matter of identifying Limits, systematically engaging them [while controlling variables], and pushing beyond previous adaptation.

We just discussed Creativity in terms of writing, but what about Creativity as a state?

In this case, the Skill Development Zone [our Limit] might represent our ability to *enter* creative states, as well as the depth and consistency in which we are able to *explore* them. In other words, we want to improve our ability to access Creativity, as well as get better at staying in that state for longer.

A huge part of accessing and using Creativity is improving your Technique and Theory so you have higher Foundations to express from. This allows you to flow with Inspiration, instead of getting caught up in 'how' you're going to express and create with it. Nothing kills Creativity more than process, procedure, and distraction. You want to focus on *being the painting*.

However, something to keep in mind, as mentioned in **Secret 13**, is that with Parkinsons' Law: work expands to fill the time allotted. This means that to push our Limits of Creativity, we first need to work within a time constraint [Practice Sprint]. This is so we can control for variables. Too short of a practice, and we can't truly recognize or push any Limits. Too long, and there are too many other potential factors that could influence our ability to access and express Creativity.

So, it's important that we optimize Creativity for smaller periods of time. Then, once we adapt, we can add on more time or further our applications to push beyond previous adaptation. By building Creativity in this way, we're building Pinnacles which become new Foundations. Our default increases.

Notice how there are some people whose 'default' level of Creativity seems so high and advanced? It's not magic or luck or natural talent. They have simply engaged with Creativity in a way that has increased their Foundation. They are able to access it quicker, explore it deeper, and express it with higher levels of Technique and Theory. So what seems like a Pinnacle to us, is simply their default; their Foundation. This is why we need to improve our ability to access as well as use Creativity. And this is done by developing Technique and Theory, and by pushing our ability to access and use Creativity within a time constraint.

To access Creativity quicker, you'll want to use routines, rituals, and anchors as described in **Secret 16**. In terms of expressing Creativity more consistently and with greater depth, you need to spend your Practice Sprints at your Limit. For example, with writing, here are some different Limits to consider:

- The speed in which you're able to create a new song, riff, or solo.
- The detail in which you're able to write a new song, riff, or solo [a basic outline versus a fully-developed part].
- The ability to implement new Techniques or Theory in a creative context.

■ The technical proficiency in which you're able to write a new song, riff, or solo [tempo, complexity, etc.]

There are obviously many more potential Limits, but this will at least give you an idea of how to engage the Skill Development Zone in terms of Creativity as a state.

I'd recommend working on these one at a time so you can control for variables and understand if you're making progress. If there are too many variables or too many outcomes you're pursuing, you'll have no idea what's working and what's not. You won't be able to make progress. And progress is our goal.

FINAL THOUGHTS

To make progress with anything you simply need to engage the Skill Development Zone. For Technique, Theory, and Creativity this is done through the Pathway to Completion sequence. However, there are other ways to engage the Skill Development Zone.

All it comes down to is identifying the Limits of what you're trying to make progress with. Then, you need to constantly engage those Limits, ideally within small, consistent time frames [while controlling for variables]. Finally, you need to fix issues [Weak Points] as they arise - continuing to push beyond previous adaptation.

The key is to have a system you follow that allows you to be consistent, control for variables, and focus your efforts around your Weak Points. This way you're not wasting time or energy in ways that aren't benefiting the outcome [Vision] you desire. You focus on what works and remove what doesn't.

This is how you build any skill or grow in any way. The only thing that changes are the particular mechanisms you need to engage with in order to identify Limits, repair Weak Points, and blast through previous adaptation. Whatever approach you choose, the focus is to remain at the edge of the Skill Development Zone for your entire session. You will be uncomfortable, but this forces adaptation and creates growth.

You don't need to practice 10 hours a day anymore to become the guitarist you've always dreamed of being. You don't need to blindly hope that what you're doing is working. You don't need to put in more time. You just need to use the time you do have better.

You need a New Framework - and this is it: The Elite Framework. Make it your Foundation.

It's all about maximizing output while minimizing input. Maximize the results of every session by minimizing the wasted time and energy that goes into them. Hyper-focus on what produces results and you will see exponential growth.

I'm sure by now your mind is flooding with endless ideas and possibilities. Good! Get excited. A whole new chapter in your life is about to open up.

It's not going to be easy, but nothing worth having or accomplishing comes easy. You'll be uncomfortable. You'll constantly push your boundaries. However, The Elite Framework, and more specifically the Pathway to Completion sequence *are* what will unlock your potential on guitar. They will allow you to become the guitarist you've always dreamed of being, without needing to practice all day.

Push your limits, engage the zone, embrace the struggle, and watch where it takes you.

HOW TO APPLY THIS

To get started with the Elite Framework, follow the Pathway to Completion sequence:

- Use a Metronome.
- **Baseline**: establish the speed in which you can comfortably perform the part correctly.

- **Encode:** properly integrate and automate the part through perfected repetition.

- **Progress:** incrementally increase the tempo while Encoding at each new level.

- **Limit:** stop when you begin making a few small mistakes.

- **Focus Shift:** focus on one mistake at a time. Repeat the previous steps at a smaller Level of Resolution.

- If you struggle getting past your Limit, use a Limit Breaker.

- Repeat this sequence as needed until...

- **Reintegration:** once the issue is correct and built up to the previous Baseline, reintegrate it with surrounding material at that level.

- Once all parts of the whole are fixed, and at your original Baseline, use the previous steps to build up to your target speed [if you aren't already there].

Ultimately our goal is to optimize our entire session around the Skill Development Zone. We need to get uncomfortable. We need to push our Limits, identify Weak Points, Encode the correct patterns and engage the edge to push beyond previous adaptation.

Whether it's Technique, Theory, or Creativity, by working in small periods of time [Practice Sprints], we're able to push harder, control for variables, and understand what's working and what's not. This is how we extract the most benefit from each second of practice, allowing us to make more progress in a month than most people would make in a year. It's all about engaging the Skill Development Zone, and one of the best ways to do that is through the Pathway to Completion sequence.

> **Practice Hacker Tip:** Make The Elite Framework your Foundation and constantly engage the Skill Development Zone to break past previous adaptation and become the guitarist you've always dreamed of being.

BOOK IV

THE GUITARIST'S GUIDE TO TOTAL PRACTICE OPTIMIZATION: BIOHACKS AND BLASTING THROUGH PLATEAUS

TRACKING. ANALYSIS. GROWTH

Secret 18

Breaking Through

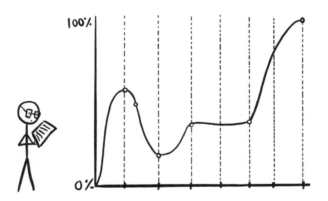

You can't make progress if you don't track the process. Progress isn't linear. The quicker you can recognize its flow, the quicker you can adjust and pivot. Be aware, track your progress, and optimize to continue your growth.

Ever since I was 2 years old, jumping in front of my TV pretending I was Ace Frehley from KISS, I had a Vision: I was going to be a great guitarist one day, on that stage, impacting people with my music. As I grew older, that desire grew stronger. I just *knew* it would happen. I had no idea *how* it would happen, but I just knew it would. The problem is that this way of thinking was nearly the cause of me quitting music altogether.

Let me explain. I always had a Vision, yes. I always had a dream. However, I never cared to know *how* I would get there. I never had a plan. I never knew if what I was doing was actually working. I just figured it would happen one day - that it would just work out, that I would just *know*. This way of thinking spilled over into every area of my life.

When I first started working out, I would go to the gym and do random exercises, but I never knew if what I was doing was actually working. When I was trying to make progress on guitar, I would practice all day long, but I never knew if what I was doing was actually working. Even in terms of my finances, I never really paid attention to my income or expenses, I just assumed things would work out, but I never knew if what I was doing was actually working.

Notice a pattern?

I never knew if what I was doing was actually working. At least... until it was too late. I wasn't Tracking anything. I wasn't analyzing anything. I wasn't improving my Foundation. I wasn't aware of my Limits or how to break through them. No plan. No clear pathway towards my destination. No way to know if I needed to change course, adapt, or pivot.

How would I ever get to where I wanted to go if I had no idea if I was even moving in the right direction? Or if I was moving at all? Have you ever felt this way?

As we know, having clear Goals towards your Vision is critical. But what is the point of having Goals if you don't know if you're even making progress? This is often where many people get stuck. This is where I was stuck, for a long time. Tracking your progress is almost more important than having the Goals themselves. The better you get at this, the quicker you can make adjustments and continue your progress. You don't want to continue doing the same thing for 10 years hoping that something will eventually change. You want to focus on what produces results.

Once I started properly Tracking my progress, everything finally opened up for me. I didn't have to wait months or even years to know if what I was doing was working. I could see, in real time, what was working and what wasn't. I could make modifications quickly to continue my growth. This awareness changed everything for me. This was the final, missing piece.

To truly open up your potential with guitar and with life, you need to track and analyze what you're doing. You need to focus on what's producing results and improve it, while also removing or modifying what isn't. If you can master this process, you'll truly become unstoppable. You'll have total freedom on guitar; easily becoming the guitarist you've always dreamed of being without needing to practice all day. You'll be able to make more progress in 1 month than most people make in 1 year. All of this, and so much more awaits you, but you need to track, analyze, and optimize your progress.

This is the final Practice Secret of the Pros - and none of the other Secrets mean anything without this one. The quicker you master this, the quicker you accelerate your pathway to mastery. This is what separates the average from the extraordinary. This is what creates elite guitarists.

Become aware. Raise your Foundations. Track your progress. Adapt as needed. Blast through plateaus. And become the guitarist you've always dreamed of being.

No excuses. Take action.

PROGRAM LENGTH

The Old Framework is focused on the 'what' of learning [Technique, Theory, exercises, songs, patterns, etc.] without an optimized system to effectively learn or practice them. So to make progress it takes countless hours of practice that *eventually* compound over time.

This is because the Skill Development Zone is usually only engaged for 3-6 minutes on average, per 60-minute session. Yes, it's better than nothing, but it's going to take a long time to compound that progress into something meaningful. However, The Elite Framework presents us with a clear and effective system to push the Skill Development Zone for the entire session. As a result, we hyper-focus the way we are practicing, which allows us to maximize our progress, quickly, without needing to practice all day long.

The beautiful part of The Elite Framework is that it's predicated on quickly finding Limits, fixing Weak Points, and pushing beyond previous adaptation - so actually hitting a plateau won't happen as often as with the Old Framework. However, it still happens. To address this issue, we want to take the core ethos of The Elite Framework and apply it to our programming as a whole.

In this book, you've been learning a lot of new concepts. I don't want you to feel overwhelmed. The best way to begin integrating them is by working within time constraints. You don't want to do too much at once. Add 1 thing at a time, or as needed and track your results. The goal is to internalize each concept so it becomes a natural part of how you approach guitar, and life. You're rebuilding your Foundation. Ensure it's as strong as possible so you can build beyond the clouds.

This is why I recommend a program length of 8 weeks. Yes, you can do a bit less or a bit more. But by having an 8-week time constraint, it allows us to build a Habit, identify our Limits, and optimize to further our growth.

We want to become effective with our time. Too short of a program, and we'll be focused on *what* we should be doing, instead of just doing it. We won't be able to truly understand or push our Limits. With too long of a program, work expands to fill the time allotted. We won't be able to truly know what we're capable of. This creates the illusion that we need *more* time to accomplish something than is actually needed.

Start with an 8-week program. Set Goals in 8-week increments. If you master your Goal in less than 8 weeks, that's great - set a bigger Goal for yourself next time, or include additional Goals. If it takes longer, then keep that in mind for future Goals and make adjustments as needed.

As you start to set Goals and begin accomplishing them, you'll gain Achievement Momentum. You'll come to understand what you're capable of and will aspire to set greater and greater Goals. This is fantastic, however I still recommend working in 8-week chunks. Even if you have larger, 1-2+ year Goals, I still recommend working on them in 8-week chunks. The more you can optimize for smaller periods of time, and stay focused on the task at hand, the more you'll be able to accomplish, and the quicker you'll be able to do so.

With all of this, we're improving our ability to self-regulate. This means we'll get better at identifying problems, we'll be able to fix them quicker, and we'll understand what tools are best to push past previous adaptation. Becoming a master of self-regulation will transform you into a truly elite musician.

TRACKING

The key to making progress is understanding what works and what doesn't. Then you want to focus your efforts on optimizing and improving what's producing results. This maximizes output, while minimizing input. This allows us to make massive amounts of progress without wasting time and energy. Then, when we hit our Limit, we simply need to make the correct adjustments and modifications to break past adaptation. But we cannot do this, unless we're aware of our progress.

Remember, music practice is a form of self-regulated learning. The better we become at self-regulation, the quicker we can make changes, therefore the quicker we can make progress. It's really that simple. We have The Elite Framework, now we need to ensure we continue growing while we use it. To accomplish this, we need to track our progress.

There are many ways to track progress, but find what works best for you. For most people, I'd recommend a journal or an app such as Evernote. Regardless, we will divide Tracking into 3 main timeframes: Daily, Weekly, and Monthly.

With each type of Tracking, I recommend addressing two different factors: your *State* and your *Performance*.

DAILY TRACKING

STATE

One of the focuses in Preparing for Practice is accessing our Ideal State [Mental]. This is because we want to be at peak levels of resourcefulness and Productivity.

So at the end of the session, note how you felt it went. How was your state going into practice, as well as during and after? Pay attention to what factors might have influenced your state.

You might ask yourself questions like:

- How did I prepare for practice?
- Did I access my Ideal State [Mental]?
- What was my emotional state?
- What was my level of focus?
- How were my energy levels?
- Was I motivated today?
- Was I distracted today?
- Was I happy, sad, stressed, etc.?

These are simply example questions. Ask yourself whatever is relevant to you, your state, and your practice. Be as detailed as you can. The more information you have, the better adjustments you can make later on.

PERFORMANCE

Your state is directly linked to your ability to perform. This is why it's critical to not only access your Ideal State [Mental], but also your Ideal State [Physical] - creating Ideal State [Synergy].

After your practice session, ask yourself questions such as:

- Did I increase my speed from the last session?
- Did I meet my target or Checkpoint today?
- Did I overcome a certain issue or Weak Point I've been struggling with?
- Did I discover a new issue I need to address?
- Did I warm-up effectively?
- Did I feel locked in, or did I struggle to play today?

Again, these are just examples. Ask yourself questions that relate to you. Be as detailed as you can.

The purpose of this is to be aware of the state you're in when you approach practice and how that correlates with your performance. By collecting and reviewing this data, we'll be able to more accurately see trends and then we can focus on what produces results while minimizing or removing what doesn't.

See why Tracking is so important?

Rate your Daily practice session out of 10.

- 0 = worst practice you've ever had
- 10 = practice perfection

WEEKLY TRACKING

At the end of each Week, review your Daily sessions for that Week. Create an average across all days of practice, **how did your Week rate out of 10?**

STATE

At the end of the week, note if there was a consistent theme or any obvious issues you need to address. On the days that you struggled with your state, what could you have done to turn those days around, especially as it relates to your practice? What other questions can you ask yourself?

Remember - don't make excuses, find ways to improve and benefit. This starts with being honest with yourself, followed by taking action, and adjusting when needed. If you do need to make adjustments, decide on 1 variable to test for the next week and track your results. Don't change too many things, you need to control for variables.

PERFORMANCE

Repeat the same process but for your performance. Are there any consistent themes or issues that you need to address? What can you do to fix them? How did your state relate to your performance? What other questions can you ask yourself?

Again, if you need to make adjustments, focus on 1 change at a time so you can actually understand what's working or not. Otherwise you'll simply waste time and energy, which is the opposite of what we're trying to do.

MONTHLY TRACKING

At the end of each month, review your Weekly sessions. Create an average across all weeks of practice during that month - **how did your month rate out of 10?**

This is also a common Checkpoint. It's halfway [4 weeks] to your 8-week Goal. Your Checkpoints identify milestones towards your Goals. Your Tracking helps identify progress towards your Checkpoints.

Review each week and note everything you can about what worked and what didn't, both relating to your state and your performance. What can you do differently for next month? If you're making any adjustments, test 1 variable at a time and track your results.

Whether regarding Practice Sprints, program length, or even levels of Tracking, it's easy to feel overwhelmed when we are focused on the larger picture. By Tracking Daily, Weekly, and Monthly, we are aware of the whole, yet focused on the part. This allows us to more fully immerse ourselves in the process. Most importantly, it helps us get started.

Remember, the point of Tracking is to pay attention to what you're doing as you're progressing towards your Goals. It gives you awareness of what's working and what's not in real time. This means you can quickly make adjustments and continue making progress.

Don't just hope for the best. Track your progress and become aware of the process. Be in control.

PROGRESS FLOW

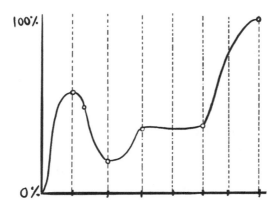

This chart was inspired by Tim Ferriss and his book '4 Hour Chef.' Progress isn't linear. If you can foresee the flow, you can more accurately address issues and attain mastery.

We often think of progress as linear, however it's anything but. When initially learning something, there is a massive upswing of progress. This is because our previous level of adaptation is pretty low. Everything is new, everything is exciting, and we're constantly engaging the Skill Development Zone.

Then, when we need to start applying this new knowledge, it becomes a bit less exciting, often stressful, and the perception we had of ourselves starts to change when we truly see our capabilities. Things become more complex and harder to navigate. We come to realize that we actually know very little. Our egos take a hit.

Without the right framework, we aren't able to continue making progress. Our 'beginner gains' wear off, and we end up practicing for hours on end without seeing any results.

Once you push through, you've established a higher, stronger Foundation for yourself. You have a bit more confidence in the basics, and you're able to build off of them - building your Foundation into Pinnacles, which then become new Foundations. You add in more complexity, more application, more nuance, and more detail. Everything becomes refined and perfected.

This process then evens out to a plateau. This is where you're working through multiple complexities, integrating everything, and really establishing your new Foundation. This Foundation is much more vast and difficult to establish - hence it appears as a plateau. No beginner gains here.

But once that new Foundation is fully established, an inflection point is achieved and the pathway to fluency/mastery begins. The problem is that most people give up before they get to this point, but not you; not the Practice Hacker. You recognize this is a part of the journey. You foresee it. You're prepared for it. You're prepared for greatness.

I don't want you to get too caught up in the details, but I do want you to understand that anything you approach on guitar and in life will have a flow like this. The better you can foresee challenges and obstacles, the better prepared you'll be to overcome them. More importantly, you'll be less likely to give up, which is the main reason most people don't succeed; they simply give up too early. Failure becomes their demise, but as stated previously, success comes after many failures. Prepare yourself for failure. Fail more. Fail better. Success awaits you around the corner.

BLAST THROUGH PLATEAUS

Now that we're aware of what to expect, and the inevitability of plateaus - how do we overcome them?

Our bodies and minds adapt to the stress we put them under, that's why they grow. Once they adapt, they aren't growing anymore so we need to add in changes to stimulate new growth.

In the context of guitar, I consider there to be 3 primary methods to overcoming plateaus:

- Rest
- Free Play
- Practice Variables

REST

This isn't referring to sleep, meditation, or relaxation [which are all important], but instead this is referring to rest days; full breaks from practicing or playing guitar. As mentioned in **Secret 14**, this should happen at the end of each 'working' period for most of us. Depending on your Daily Routine and Weekly Sequencing, this might be after 1, 2, or 3 days of consecutive practice.

If you're really optimizing and pushing your sessions, having 1 day off in-between them might not be enough. You need to take time to let your body heal. Eat well, sleep well, stretch, and get some light physical activity in. You need to recover. Once you become more advanced, you can practice for more consecutive days in a row, however rest is still a critical element. Add in extra rest days once you're noticing a plateau or decline in skill development/progress. Keep track of how it influences your practice sessions so you can use it properly in the future.

Sometimes after a very difficult and intense 8-week program, you might need an entire week off, or a week where you just do whatever you want. Listen to your body and do what's necessary for your growth, and ultimately for your health.

FREE PLAY

Let yourself have some extra fun in the week by just *playing* guitar, without any point or purpose. Depending on your schedule, this could be a few minutes a day, or a specific day of the week [like Sunday].

Free plays are already built-in to the examples given in **Secret 14**, however, add them in as needed. Guitar should be fun, don't allow it to become stale or simply a chore. If you're getting stuck or hitting Limits, sometimes just taking a day where you mess around and have fun is all you need to keep the progress flowing. You're still stimulating your mind and body, but in different ways, which can help break past plateaus.

You'll never be consistent with growth and forming a Habit if your association with practice is negative. It's okay to forget the rules sometimes. Play and do what you want!

PRACTICE VARIABLES

Practice Variables have been mentioned multiple times throughout this book. It's a simple concept: add intentional change to your routine or session in a way that provides new stimulation for growth. As they say, variety is the spice of life.

You can add in Practice Variables during your session to break past sticking points, or you can dedicate an entire session [or more] to them.

List of some Practice Variables:

- Limit Breaker [Lite]: Practice at 10-15bpm above your Baseline or target speed.
- Limit Breaker [Insanity]: Practice at double your Baseline or target speed.

- Shift to a related skill.

  - Example: alternate picking to sweep or economy picking.

- Shift to a completely different skill.

  - Example: alternate picking to tapping or fingerpicking.

- Change the speed, rhythm, note division, pulse, etc.
- Practice, focusing on different Performance Measurements or Practice Strategies.
- Practice with just the left hand independently.
- Practice with just the right hand independently.
- Press down as light as you can during your practice session.
- Press down as hard as you can during your practice session.
- Change the guitar you're playing on to one that's more difficult to play [thicker strings, higher string height, acoustic guitar, or even a bass guitar].
- Try writing or playing something with a skill that you don't fully have down yet.

  - This will help pre-wire/prime your brain to be able to do it later.

- Change the amount of work vs rest.

  - Example: working in 11-minute Practice Sprints with a 30-second Effective Break.

- Change Routine Type.
- Change Weekly Sequencing.

Brainstorm your own ways as well. Just change the stimulus every once in a while to allow progress to continue. Become aware of what works for you, and use it as often as you need to.

A focused path will bring results, but is also the cause for adaptation [hitting plateaus]. This is why it's important to build our practice sessions and programs around specific Goals, using a consistent approach and system. We need to be engaging the Skill Development Zone in a repeatable, predictable way. And most importantly, we need to control for variables. Then, once we hit a Limit [identified through Tracking], we can then use the appropriate tool [Rest, Free Play, or Practice Variables] to continue our progress.

Awareness of the process allows us to optimize it. The quicker you're aware of change needing to happen, the quicker you can address it, and consequently, the quicker you can make progress.

BUILDING STRENGTH

PHYSICAL STRENGTH

The stronger your Foundation, the further you can push yourself.

One thing that few people put much thought into is how important physical strength is to their overall health. The stronger you are physically, the more it will help most areas of your life - including guitar. Think of all of the tasks that you need to do in a day. Whether it's just moving your own body around, lifting things at your workplace, picking up or playing with your kids, working on your vehicle, mowing the lawn, cleaning, or whatever else is a part of your life - most of it requires some level of physical strength.

If you don't take care of your body, you will suffer. There's no way around it. Your body will degrade much quicker - decreasing your quality of life exponentially as you get older. You will also be more at risk for injury, sickness, and disease.

However, improving physical strength is known to increase longevity, and your overall health and wellbeing. If you take care of your health, especially as it relates to physical strength, you will be able to more fully engage with life. You'll be able to handle greater physical stress. You will be more competent. Your body will function how it's designed to. Your ability to avoid or handle injury, sickness, and disease will improve substantially. Overall, your quality of life will increase.

This doesn't mean that you need to take it to the extreme and weigh 300lbs of pure muscle. Also, ladies you aren't going to get 'bulky' if you lift weights. Just get in the gym and do some compound exercises [bench press, overhead press, deadlifts, rows, and squats]. For most people, this is all you will need. You can even start with bodyweight versions of these if a gym isn't viable for you right now.

Something as basic as a 15-20 minute full-body workout a few times a week will be plenty for most people. Just focus on building up your strength and building the Habit. This will be one of the most important things you do for yourself and for your health. This is one of the most important ways you can invest in yourself and your future.

I personally know what it's like to struggle with weight issues; having no desire to eat healthy or workout. In fact, I didn't even drink water throughout most of my childhood to teen years. All I wanted to eat was junk food and fast food. All I wanted to drink was pop. It was awful. As a result, I got *really* overweight in my early teens and suffered greatly because of it.

It took years of suffering for me to even begin wanting to change. I had to develop a big enough reason 'why.' But now, it's my lifestyle. I workout 4-5 days a week and love every moment of it. I look forward to going to the gym and my entire life, across every dimension, has improved because of it.

Suffering was the catalyst, but experiencing the benefits across each area of my life [including guitar] was the Motivation needed to establish the Habit and build the Pillars of Consistency.

Now, I'm immersed in the process of becoming more. As a result, I get to enjoy the fruits of my labour as a reward, but not the sole focus. This is what we want to develop with practice, with health, and any new Habit we're creating. Consider revisiting the information in **Secret 15** if you need more help with establishing a new Habit and creating a lifestyle around it.

If you really want to go to the next level on guitar, you need to enhance your physical strength and create a Habit around your physical health and fitness. It's not only key to living a healthy life, but also a happy, productive, and fulfilling one - truly maximizing it.

There are many great resources out there on strength training, but I highly recommend Starting Strength, 5x5 StrongLifts, or any of Jeff Nippard's programs. These resources have all benefited me greatly and I cannot speak highly enough of them. Don't overcomplicate it. Get started, build a Habit, enjoy the process, create a lifestyle, and you'll be unstoppable. Just find what works for you and what you can be consistent with - then stick with it.

FRETTING STRENGTH

Improving your physical strength enhances nearly all areas of your life. However, as guitarists, we also need to improve our fretting strength. Sometimes, this happens as a byproduct of improving our physical strength [through lifting weights], but fretting requires engaging our fingers in a different way, so it might require a different approach.

As we know with developing and building skills, we need to establish our Foundation, Encode, and build until we hit a Limit. Then, once a Limit is hit, we need to identify the issue, Encode, and repeat. For fretting, it's similar, but it more closely resembles the concept of Progressive Overload in the fitness world. In short, for our body to grow and break past previous adaptation, we need to stimulate it in new ways. We do this by adding more weight or effort to increase stimulation.

Practice Variables that increase fretting strength:

- Press down as hard as you can during a practice session.
- Change the guitar you're playing on to one that's more difficult to play [thicker strings, higher string height, acoustic guitar, or even a bass guitar].

Other ways to increase fretting strength:

- Finger strength tools or gadgets such as D'Addario's Varigrip
- Finger exercises such as the Finger Gym by JustinGuitar or as found in Rock Discipline by John Petrucci. If you choose this route, simply use The Elite Framework to work on them.

BIOHACKS

For true optimization, the pathway is two-fold: the mind and the body.

Following the protocols in this book and making them your Foundation will get you 80-90% of the way there. However, to truly maximize your potential you need to go the extra-mile. You need to optimize your physical and mental health; creating synergy that expands your potential into territories beyond your wildest imagination.

This is where Biohacking comes into play. This is the final 10-20%. This is what really separates the average from the elite.

There are different definitions for Biohacking, but they are all based around the concept of manipulating the mind and body in order to optimize performance. Some aspects of Biohacking can include more extreme measures such as genetic manipulation or even human augmentation. However, for the Practice Hacker, Biohacking is the process of making small, incremental adjustments that enhance and improve the mind and the body. Biohacking allows you to access more of your potential. It helps reprogram you for *your* benefit. It helps give you back control.

I am not a healthcare professional, nor am I giving dietary, exercise, or health advice. I am sharing, based on my own research, personal experience, and the experience of others, information that has improved my life and has allowed me to accomplish more than I ever thought possible. Make decisions based on your own research and unique circumstances. Always consult with a physician or healthcare professional when making decisions regarding diet, exercise, or health.

BRAIN STIMULATION

Read more. If you don't like reading, listen to audiobooks. Focus on developing different areas of your life; growing, learning, and becoming more. Increase your ability to think, to understand, and ultimately to create. Take notes, formulate your ideas, and connect what you learn to other areas of your life.

The reason many of us get stuck is due to not keeping up with a changing world. We are designed to grow; to evolve. If you're not growing, you're dying. The best way to grow in all areas of your life and to create the person you desire to be, is by enhancing the source of your action: your mind.

Keep your brain evolving and watch how much life opens up for you. To grow, we must nurture ourselves. To nurture ourselves, we must educate ourselves. I found the easiest way to get into this Habit is by first understanding our Vision and Beliefs. If we have a clear idea of the outcome we desire, and we believe we can accomplish it, then we're far more inspired to learn and grow along the way.

Once you know where you want to be in life, and you have a deep enough connection with that outcome, the next step is understanding what it takes to get there.

Personally, I don't read a lot of fiction. I'm not opposed to it, but it's much easier for me to read non-fiction books on business, self-improvement, marketing, finance, fitness, and other related subjects. This is because the knowledge I'm consuming applies directly to each area of my life that I'm actively working on improving. Therefore, the more I read, the more success I have. This is because I'm upgrading myself to the level needed to create my desired result; becoming the person I need to be; becoming more.

By taking the wisdom [the frameworks] of those who have the results we want and making it our Foundation, there's really no Limit to what we can achieve. To me, this is incredibly exciting and liberating. It breathes new potential into life. Nothing is fixed. Anything is possible.

I wouldn't recommend approaching anything, including reading or education, in a disjointed fashion. You want to ensure that what you're focusing on is the most likely way to achieve your desired outcome. If you're reading or educating yourself in a way that's unrelated to your Goals, it might not be enough of an incentive to maintain Consistency.

Remember, your brain wants to move away from pain and towards pleasure. If you associate enough pleasure with this new task, by seeing how it enhances and improves different areas of your life, then not doing it would cause you more pain than the pain you might experience trying something new.

At the end of the day, you want to continue upgrading and evolving your mind. In my opinion, the best way to do this is through consuming content like books and audiobooks related to your Goals and Vision. Additionally, courses, consulting, and mentorship help you go even further along this path, and quicker. They just require a greater investment.

Find what works best for you, as long as you're evolving your mind. If you're not growing, you're dying.

HEALTHY HORMONES AND BRAIN FUNCTION

Based on my research and understanding, Saturated Fat, Omega-3 Fatty Acids, and Cholesterol are key components for a healthy brain. These also greatly benefit Myelination and Neurogenesis as well as other cell and hormone functions. Whenever possible, consume these from clean food sources, not processed ones, and try to avoid Trans Fats.

INFLAMMATION

Though we experience inflammation physically through soreness, tightness, and other related ailments, it also affects us mentally. It causes brain fog, impairs quality of thinking, and decreases cognitive function - among other things. It's even been found to influence anxiety and depression in many people. Some ways to reduce inflammation are:

- Remove or limit processed foods.
- Limit sugar intake [especially processed sugar].
- Consider adding [high-quality] curcumin and black pepper to your diet.
- Limit your Omega-6 Fatty Acid intake and increase your Omega-3 Fatty Acid intake.

    - The ideal Omega-6:Omega-3 ratio is 1:1 [the Western Diet is about 15:1 to 17:1 for contrast].

CLEAN WATER

I cannot overemphasize the importance of clean water. If there is one area of your nutrition you should focus on, this is probably it. It doesn't have to be expensive, but ensure you drink purified water with no fluoride or harsh chemicals in it. Ideally, you want RO [Reverse Osmosis] water. However, if the water has been completely stripped of minerals, this can also cause issues, so you will want to reintroduce minerals for your body to absorb. Also, you don't want water that's too acidic - a pH of 6-8.5 is ideal.

Try adding minerals/electrolytes back to your filtered water. You can do this by adding something like a pinch of Pink Himalayan Salt to it. Start your day by hydrating. Include this in your morning routine. Drinking water - high quality water, will improve your health across so many dimensions. I don't think this needs to be elaborated on much further. Drink high quality, remineralized water.

FASTING

It has been shown that fasting helps regenerate stem cells in the body, allowing the body to heal in ways it normally isn't able to when constantly digesting or processing food or drinks. This is known as Autophagy.

For most, intermittent fasting is enough to not only encourage this process but also help regulate eating times. This aids in decreasing overall caloric consumption, in turn helping with weight/fat loss as an added benefit. I found for myself that an 8-hour window for eating is generally easy to sustain [from 12pm to 8pm for example]. Ensure you're still eating enough food to get your daily nutritional requirements [especially if you're including exercise or other activities].

EXERCISE

We have gone over exercise quite a bit throughout this book, but physical fitness aids mental fitness. Cardio and strength training are key components of a healthy mind and body. Additionally, flexibility and overall functionality are very important as well. It's my Belief that to get the most out of life, we should augment the natural versus going against it. This means we should be engaging our mind and body in the ways they were designed for, even if the applications in the modern, technological age are a bit different than that of our ancestors. Ultimately, find what allows you to live life to its fullest.

We know that physical strength [and muscle] improves longevity. It also allows for the ability to accomplish physical tasks easier. You get more out of life when you can better engage it. Whether you travel, play with your kids, want to learn new skills, work, or desire to maximize your enjoyment of life - physical strength plays a key role. As an added benefit, you also develop discipline, which helps improve other areas of your life - unlocking more of your potential.

Aside from the obvious physical benefits, strength training positively affects the brain as well. By increasing hormone production, it triggers changes in brain structure and function. Some of this change includes forming new brain cells, creating stronger connections, and developing new blood vessels which provide your brain with oxygen and essential nutrients. It also increases the size of certain areas of your brain, which enhances mind function. It's even been found that strength training can help improve or alleviate some symptoms of depression and anxiety. As we can see, strength training is immensely important.

Additionally, cardiovascular training is a great way to slow the loss of brain tissue over time; improving cognitive performance. Cardiovascular training has many other benefits as well, such as improving heart health, lowering blood pressure, reducing chronic pain, regulating blood sugar, regulating weight, strengthening your immune system, and improving your quality of sleep. It can also help you quickly release tension and recover from mental exhaustion.

However, something less known is that by optimizing your HRV [Heart Rate Variability], it will greatly enhance your ability to recover in-between periods of work. This means you'll be able to control and enter deeper states of focus, flow, and relaxation on command. This is especially useful when needing to access your Ideal State before recording, before performing, or during any other point of stress or pressure in which you need to be at your best. This can be achieved through forms High Intensity Interval Training [HIIT].

Flexibility is also very important. Lack of flexibility can be an indication of inflammatory issues, but it also puts you at a higher risk for injury. Having your body able to move and stretch without limitation will increase blood flow [increasing nutrient absorption], decrease inflammation, improve posture, prevent injuries, release tension, relax the mind, and increase overall energy.

Exercise, as we can see, is not simply a 1-dimensional task, but rather a multi-dimensional one. Making it a part of your lifestyle will improve every area of your life, exponentially.

Remember: augment the natural. Whatever you do, ensure you're taking care of your #1 asset: you. Investing in yourself [your mental and physical health] is the best investment you will ever make. Your future, and those you're meant to impact depend on it.

MORNING ROUTINE

Consider developing a morning routine that establishes an empowering mindset and helps you gain control over your state. Additionally, if you include high-leverage tasks like guitar practice, fitness, or working on your most important Goals, it will not only set your day up for success, but will also set up the rest of your life for success. This is being proactive. No matter what happens in a day, we're taking care of our needs and building towards a better tomorrow.

As we know, many people in life are reactive - and their results speak for themselves. They go to bed late, they wake up late, they barely get themselves together, then go to work, school, or tend to whatever else life throws at them. They don't take the time to work on themselves; creating the person they desire to be.

They simply go out in the world, give it what it requires from them, and then any free time they get is usually spent watching TV, on social media, playing video games, or something similar. On their own, these things aren't inherently negative - we all enjoy decompressing in our own way. But it becomes dangerous when it's our only form of escape, because the rest of our life is out of our control, and we aren't the person we want, or need to be to change it.

This is why we need to regain control of our lives. We need to be able to move forward. We need to become a producer of the world around us, not a product of it.

One of the best ways to do this, is by creating and following a morning routine.

Your morning routine may include:

- Making your Bed
- Drinking Water
- Making Tea or Coffee
- Guitar Practice
- Working on your Goals
- Meditation/Visualization
- Deep Breathing
- Cold Showers/Ice Baths
- Supplements
- Reading
- Inspirational Stimulation [music, videos, images]
- Affirmations/Prayer
- Exercise [running, weights, yoga, stretching]
- Vision/Goal Review
- Anchors
- etc.

Don't make it complicated. Don't add too many things at once.

Start with 1 item at a time, build a Habit around it, fall in love with the process, enjoy the benefits, and then add more as you desire. Remember, with all of this we are looking to focus on what produces our desired results. Then, we want to repeat its use and further optimize it. Whether with guitar practice itself, getting into our Ideal State, Biohacking, or really anything else, the end-goal is the same: maximize output while minimizing input. Focus on what creates your desired results, and eliminate the rest.

Your morning routine might only be 10 minutes long, or it could be 60. Whatever it is, ensure you are consistent. As we know, the Pillars of Consistency build the temple.

Start small - but start.

EVENING ROUTINE

A lot of people struggle with insomnia or even just poor sleep quality. It's suggested that blue-light [cellphones, computers, etc.] before bed affects your body's natural sleep cycle and rhythms.

A morning routine is limited by the quality of sleep going into it. If you're sleep-deprived, a morning routine will only help you so much.

Consider an evening routine 1-2 hours before bed. Some ideas might include:

- Restricting use of technology/phones/screens
- Reading
- Meditation
- Reflection

You can further optimize your sleep by keeping your room at a slightly cool temperature, using pillows/blankets that enhance sleep quality, and cutting out caffeine 4-6 hours before bedtime. You might also consider using different types of light therapy to improve the quality of your sleep.

SUPPLEMENTATION

Ideally, the bulk of your diet and nutrition should be natural, whole foods. This is what we're designed to eat. This will get you most of the way there. However, as Practice Hackers, we want to maximize output. We want to get the absolute most out of life, as well as music. This means, once we have a strong Foundation, we might want to expand off of it; augmenting the natural. Things to consider adding:

- Natural Nootropics
- Vitamins/minerals [such as D3, B12, and even Omega-3 if you're deficient]
- Creatine
- Caffeine + L-Theanine
- Bulletproof Coffee/Tea
- Etc.

Again, find what works best for you. There is no one-size-fits-all approach. Ensure you develop a strong Foundation, and then if you find ways that help improve beyond that - perfect. As always, I recommend only sticking with what's natural, and always consult a Doctor or healthcare professional before making any dietary, exercise, or health changes.

You want to focus on health and longevity. Don't try to take shortcuts that could harm you. Optimize your mind and body to provide the Foundation your need to become the guitarist you've always dreamed of being.

HELL OR HEALTH

Years ago, my entire life was built around destructive habits. For most of my childhood and youth, *all* I ate was fast food, sweets, chips, snacks, chocolates, and ice cream. When I say that's all I ate, I'm not exaggerating. I didn't touch a vegetable. I didn't really eat fruit. I rarely ate home-cooked meals - and when I did, they certainly weren't healthy. I never consumed water, but I did drink a *lot* of pop and sugary juice.

I would stay up all night playing video games and conversely I would sleep all day. I wasn't doing anything to improve myself - and my health and music abilities were declining. I was overweight. I had bad acne. My teeth were falling apart. However, this was only the beginning. This lifestyle evolved into even more destructive behaviours. I won't go into the details here, but let's just say this eventually led to a very serious life or death situation which caused me to reevaluate everything.

As extreme as this situation was, it seemed to be the suffering I needed to experience in order to finally push my life in the right direction. From then on, I became obsessed with health and improving myself on all levels. I hope that you don't need such a drastic wake-up call if you're stuck in destructive patterns and behaviours right now. Not everyone makes it. This is actually a huge reason as to why I wrote this book.

I could've easily just written a book around effective guitar practice, but all of that is actually a very small part of becoming a great guitarist; the guitarist you've always dreamed of being. It's really about diving into your own life and creating the person you want to be; the person you're destined to be. Guitar is simply a facet of that, it's an expression, it's a tool.

The journey is about becoming your potential; about becoming more. It's about carving out your unique path in the world. It's about living a life of excellence - whatever that means to you. Guitar, and music are vessels to express and communicate this, but ultimately they are extensions of *you*. The more developed *you* are, it not only improves the quality of your life, and the lives of those around you, but it also greatly enhances your music abilities.

In my new-found passion for health, I tested numerous diets, lifestyles, supplements, superfoods, exercise - you name it. All I knew is that I wanted to be healthy. What came as a surprise though, is that when I began taking better care of my mind and body, my Creativity improved. I found I could access it more consistently. I could go deeper. Ideas were connecting in ways I hadn't seen before. Most importantly - I had the energy, focus, and ability to execute these new ideas.

It's funny looking back now. I didn't realize at the time that all of these things were connected. I guess you don't know what you don't know...

In making myself healthier, and engaging with the protocols I've mentioned in this chapter, and in fact throughout this book, I unlocked an entirely new potential within myself. It actually felt like a veil had been lifted; like I was seeing life for the first time. I felt like this potential was always there, but it seemed hidden - only popping up occasionally in moments of Inspiration or Creativity. However, when I made these changes, this potential became my default; my Foundation.

Up until that point, I hated reading, learning, physical activity, healthy eating, etc. But once I had a big enough reason to change, my life completely turned around. Those things I once hated, quickly became my new lifestyle. All of this transformed me into a new person; a better person, with a stronger Vision and the ability to finally cultivate it.

We can have the best systems, we can have the best tools, but if we're limited in our ability to use them [mind and body] - our potential and our impact become limited.

Who wants to live a limited life? Not me. Not you. Not the Practice Hacker.

It also doesn't help that we hold this image of guitarists and musicians as 'rock stars.' That their great accomplishments are strictly because of their lifestyle. What people don't realize is that they are simply accessing states. The issue is that these states are very short-lived and unsustainable. They burn bright, but burnout quickly.

Practice Hackers seek longevity and consistency. We seek to be in control of our state. We are a new breed of musician. By taking a new approach, we can inspire a new generation of musicians who seek to improve themselves and impact the world with their music.

Take care of your mind and body. They are the Foundation on which everything you do is possible.

**Your Vision will decide where you can go.
Your Foundation will decide if you can get there.**

HOW TO APPLY THIS

Set Goals in 8-week increments. This will allow you enough time to build a Habit and identify your Limits so you can optimize to further your growth. Too short of a program or too long, and you'll run into problems which will hold you back from accomplishing your Goals, and ultimately your Vision.

Ensure that you're Tracking Daily, Weekly, and Monthly to be aware of what's working and what isn't. Note your State and your Performance.

Plateaus are inevitable, even with The Elite Framework. Utilize Rest days, Free Play, or Practice Variables to break past points of adaptation and continue your growth.

Finally, always be raising your Foundation; the health of your mind and body. This is critical. As you continue strengthening and building your Foundation, you can utilize Biohacks to further enhance your performance.

Whether with the 8-week program or Practice Sprints, the focus is to get the absolute most out of our sessions, without wasting time or energy. Remember: we need to maximize output while minimizing input. To do this, we need to work within time constraints and repeat the same [or similar] protocols for each session. We need to be consistent. This develops a solid Foundation for our practice, which allows us to control for variables.

As we build a Habit and start identifying and pushing our Limits, we can test different variables to see what allows us to break past adaptation and what doesn't. If we are working on too many Goals at once, or our practice routines are too sporadic and inconsistent, then we don't really know if what we're doing is working. It's nearly impossible to make accurate assessments or adjustments.

The quicker you can identify issues, the quicker you can make corrections. This means you'll be able to continue making progress instead of getting stuck for days, weeks, months, or even years.

Don't get overwhelmed by the idea of making changes. The bigger you make them out to be, the more difficult it will be to not only start, but to be consistent enough to form a Habit. Stay focused on your Vision. Develop a strong Foundation. Develop Consistency. Make small adjustments and track their effects. Focus on what's working and further improve it. Remove what isn't working, or modify it to work.

Any changes you decide to make regarding diet, exercise, or health should be consulted with a Doctor or healthcare professional.

At the end of the day, find what works best for you and allows you to become the guitarist you've always dreamed of being.

Practice Hacker Tip: Optimize your mind and your body to maximize your potential in every way. Be aware of the process, track your progress, and add in Practice Variables as needed to ensure you continue to grow.

CONCLUSION

Secret 19

Tying it all Together

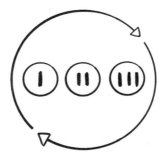

The Practice Secrets of the Pros allow you to create the results you've always desired on guitar. There are 3 distinct phases that you'll start with and revisit along your pathway to guitar mastery.

What a journey this has been, and I couldn't be more appreciative that we're embarked on it together.

First off, I want to thank you for showing interest in this book and taking action to improve yourself as a guitarist and as a person. It's a huge step. Most people simply hope and dream for a better life, never taking action - but not you. I respect you for that.

As I've mentioned throughout this book, these Practice Secrets of the Pros came together as the result of me nearly giving up guitar and music.

To most, that might not seem like much, but for me it was everything. Since I was 2 years old, I knew that I was going to be a great guitarist one day, on that stage, impacting people with my music. It was my identity; it was my purpose; it was my destiny. Yet, it was falling apart right before my eyes.

I truly believed that because I couldn't make progress on guitar, I wouldn't be able to become the guitarist I've always dreamed of being. As a result, I wouldn't be able to create the songs I always wanted to create. I wouldn't be able to tour or be on stage. I wouldn't be able to impact others with my music. I wouldn't be able to teach others. I wouldn't even be able to learn the songs or riffs that I loved listening to.

I also believed that I wouldn't be able to move forward with my life. I had spent my entire life working towards this. So much time, energy, and money. If I couldn't make *this* happen, how would I be able to do anything else?

I couldn't give up. I needed to do whatever it took. That decision led me on a journey that's been nothing short of incredible. It really opened me up to an entirely new way of seeing and experiencing life. It showed me that anything is possible, you just need the right system; the right framework to do it. You need to become the person capable of creating the results you desire. You *can* change yourself. You *can* improve yourself. Nothing is fixed. You can always become more.

Through this transformative process, I discovered and synthesized the Practice Secrets of the Pros - the system responsible for turning the average guitarist into the guitarist they've always dreamed of being, without needing to practice all day.

However, this system is so much more than that. It's the system for becoming the *person* you've always dreamed of being. It really applies to everything in life.

The core of this book is The Elite Framework. This is initially what I was searching for - the way to finally make progress on guitar without sacrificing my entire life to practice. I could've easily just written a short book on The Elite Framework and put it out into the world, but I realized I would actually be doing a disservice to you and everyone else.

The Elite Framework is simply a mechanism. But to become the guitarist we've always dreamed of being, it requires an entire paradigm shift. This is where the rest of the Practice Secrets of the Pros come into play. We need to break free from the chains of the Old Framework. We need to take back control. We need to become the person capable of creating the results we desire. We need to become more.

What do the world's most successful people, in any field, have in common?

They aspire for greatness - they hunger for it. They understand how to build their skills and how to engage their Skill Development Zone. They have the Mindset and Beliefs to support their Vision. They understand how to set Goals and develop Consistency to achieve them. They are masters of self-regulation. They know how to access their Ideal State to create their highest level of resourcefulness and Productivity. They know how to track their progress, optimize, and blast through plateaus. They are in control. They take action.

I now live by these principles; the Practice Secrets of the Pros. They have been the lessons and knowledge that have transformed my life. They have given me the tools to become the person and guitarist I've always dreamed of being. They've allowed me to create results I didn't even know I was capable of creating. They've allowed me to take control of my destiny, all without wasting time, energy, or money.

Now, they are yours. You hold the key. You hold the secrets. The rest is up to you.

You might be asking yourself: *'What do I do next?'*

This book should be seen more as a playbook. It should be revisited and referenced often. Don't try too many new things at once. Develop your Foundation - internalize the basics. Build off of them, adding 1 new thing at a time if needed. Focus on what works and remove what doesn't.

Optimize. Expand. Repeat.

We can consider this book to have 3 separate phases:

PHASE I [Preparation]:

- Establish your Mindset and Beliefs.
- Create your Vision [Macro/Micro].
- Create your Goals.
- Choose your Routine and Sequencing.

PHASE II [Execution]:

- Create your Ideal State [Synergy].
- Use The Elite Framework to Work on your Goals.

PHASE III [Expansion]:

- Track your Progress [Daily, Weekly, and Monthly].
- Break through Plateaus.

Whether you've played guitar for 30 years or 30 days, this book will provide you the Foundation you need to become the guitarist you've always dreamed of being. And you won't need to practice all day long. The Old Framework has failed us. It wastes hundreds of our precious hours, and thousands of our hard earned dollars a year, and for what? To be at the same place we've always been? Thinking we just need to practice *more*? That maybe we aren't good enough? That we'll never be more than we are?

So many guitarists with incredible potential give up before they ever get the chance to impact others with their music. For each person who gives up on their purpose; on their unique contribution to this life, the world becomes a darker place. I believe it's my mission to help reverse that; to help make the world a brighter and better place. To help others realize their potential and connect to their path. I believe musicians and creative individuals have the power to change the world. Music and art have a greater effect on culture than any institution, government, or media could ever have.

Whatever we've been doing before needs to change. It's not working. We need a new way of thinking. A new approach to practice. A new way of developing and sharpening our skills. A new way to fulfill our purpose and pursue our dreams. A new way of cultivating a better version of ourselves. Something not restricted to a select few, but that anyone can use to create exceptional results.

And that's why I created Practice Secrets of the Pros. I believe this is how we can change. I believe this is how we can unlock our potential, impact others with our music, and create a better world. Make this your Foundation. Whatever you choose to build upon it is up to you. Now, go out there and take action. Whatever you want out of guitar and life, go and get it. I believe in you - I truly do. I cannot wait to see what Practice Secrets of the Pros does for you.

Please feel free to hit me up on social media and let me know what secrets have changed your life!

Your friend and fellow Practice Hacker,

Coco Lee

PS. You're Only One Practice Away...